Literature
Review

LONGEVITY RISK AND
RETIREMENT INCOME
PLANNING

Patrick J. Collins, CFA, Huy D. Lam, CFA, and Josh Stampfli

CFA Institute
Research
Foundation

Statement of Purpose

The CFA Institute Research Foundation is a not-for-profit organization established to promote the development and dissemination of relevant research for investment practitioners worldwide.

Cover Image Photo Credit: iStock.com/Kemter

ISBN 978-1-934667-95-8

28 December 2015

Editorial Staff

Mary-Kate Hines
Editor

Abby Farson Pratt
Assistant Editor

Cindy Maisannes
Manager, Publications Production

Tracy Dinning
Senior Publishing Technology Specialist

Contents

CE Qualified Activity CFA Institute   This publication qualifies for 3.5 CE credits under the guidelines of the CFA Institute Continuing Education Program.

Longevity Risk and Retirement Income Planning

Patrick J. Collins, CFA
Schultz Collins, Inc.

Huy D. Lam, CFA
Schultz Collins, Inc.

Josh Stampfli
Independent Consultant

Introduction

Over the past 50 years, there has been an accretion of research on the topic of longevity risk and portfolio sustainability from scholars and practitioners in diverse fields.

- *Actuaries* are interested in the factors that determine the pricing of contracts that guarantee lifetime income.

- *Financial economists* are interested in building models that reflect the evolution of retirement portfolios under the stress of expenses and withdrawals and in using models to optimize outcomes expressed in both dollar-wealth and utility terms.

- *Investment advisers* are interested in how best to advise clients on a variety of retirement and intergenerational wealth management issues.

- *Trustees* charged with providing lifetime income to current beneficiaries and terminal wealth to remaindermen are interested in how to fulfill their fiduciary duties prudently and impartially.

- *Investors* are interested in how much money they can safely spend, give, or bequeath from their retirement portfolio.

Not only is the volume of research vast, but the range of publications also reflects pedagogy from academic fields that traditionally have little overlap in readership. Although hundreds of authors have contributed to our understanding of how retirement income portfolios behave in the presence of distributions, we limit the focus primarily, although not exclusively, to academic studies—not because the numerous articles appearing in trade-oriented publications lack value but because the academic literature is, for the most part, free of sales and marketing agendas. As such, it represents an independent, objective source of credible information. A more comprehensive and technically detailed literature survey, arranged in chronological order, is available in Collins (2015). It comments extensively on both academic and practitioner-oriented literature.

This review, however, is organized both chronologically and thematically. Its focus is on research studies that model and evaluate portfolio design, implementation, and management strategies for producing adequate lifetime income for retired investors. Unless otherwise indicated, it does not consider wealth accumulation during the investor's pre-retirement working years. Where appropriate, the survey also extends to literature that considers gifting and bequest objectives.

Four supplemental literature surveys, in addition to this review, might prove useful: Shapiro (2010); Crawford, de Haan, and Runchey (2008); MacDonald, Jones, Morrison, Brown, and Hardy (2013); and Milevsky (2013).[1]

Any summary of mathematically complex articles must inevitably result in oversimplifications that, to the authors of such articles, may seem to distort their work. Although we offer no defense against this charge other than good faith, we nevertheless suspect that the benefit of presenting, in relatively non-technical language, a broad survey of research articles outweighs any embedded faults. Readers wishing to explore the mathematics underlying academic research will find a greater level of technical explication in Collins (2015). Of course, there is no substitute for reading the original research.

Research conclusions are byproducts of mathematical models. Although academic insights derived from these models influence economic theory, they are less likely to contribute to normative economics. Research models often incorporate both simplifying assumptions and mathematical approaches in order to become tractable. This observation simply acknowledges that models yield benefits—insights into how critical variables interact—and manifest limitations. A research study's conclusions do not necessarily translate into investment-planning prescriptions for actual investors.

---

[1]The Society of Actuaries sponsored the first three studies. They are on the society's website (www.soa.org).

Themes and Structure of the Literature Review

Longevity Risk

Longevity risk is the economic consequences of outliving a portfolio of financial assets tasked with providing lifetime income. The US Social Security Administration's general population mortality table evidences an increase in the percentage of the adult population surviving until age 65. The percentage of males in the 1940 cohort surviving from age 21 to age 65 is 53.9%; the percentage of females is 60.6%. For the 1990 cohort, the percentages adjust to 72.3% and 83.6%, respectively. Thus, a greater percentage of the general population is living to retirement age. The average remaining life expectancy for those surviving to age 65 is 12.7/14.7 years for the male/female 1940 cohort, and 15.3/19.6 years for the male/female 1990 cohort.[2]

Within the blue-collar population group, there is an emerging and well-documented retirement crisis. Primary economic reasons include the decline of defined benefit pension plans, a discomfort with investing in higher expected return assets (a variation on a financial illiteracy explanation), and stagnation in real wage growth leading to difficulty in accumulating pre-retirement wealth. Within the high-income, white-collar population group, it is not uncommon for one or more spouses to live beyond age 90.[3] This means that an investment portfolio may have a planning horizon greater than 35 years assuming an investor in his or her mid-60s. Additionally, this latter population group often has a high standard of living, which may require substantial cash flows to continue unabated throughout one's lifespan. In a low-yield environment, traditional fixed-income-oriented strategies for providing adequate and sustainable income are under pressure because of the desire to maintain established lifestyles.

Actuarial Solutions vs. Investment Solutions

Some authors assert that capital market volatility calls into question the viability of using risky-asset portfolios to generate stable periodic cash flows throughout a long-term horizon. Risky-asset portfolio values may decrease; a retiree's need for cash flow certainty may not. Although long-term expected returns from stocks may remain attractive, a sequence of negative returns can

---

[2]See www.ssa.gov/history/lifeexpect.html.
[3]Mortality data are based on the recent mortality experience of 123 uninsured US private and public retirement plans are available in the Society of Actuaries "RP-2014 Mortality Tables Report" (www.soa.org/Research/Experience-Study/pension/research-2014-rp.aspx).

deplete a retirement income portfolio to the point where it lacks sufficient dollars to recover. Retirement assets must support a growing population of long-lived investors, and unfortunately, the traditional investment-oriented methods of financing long-term cash flows appear, in the opinion of some commentators, to offer a tenuous prospect for satisfactory results.

One actuarial solution to providing income during retirement takes the form of holding life insurance contracts for the benefit of a surviving spouse and dependents. The demand to hold life insurance contracts during retirement, although an important financial planning topic, is only briefly discussed in this literature review. Rather, most attention is given to the demand to hold annuity contracts. In general, the literature discusses annuities in one of three contexts:

1. As actuarial alternatives to maintaining a portfolio exclusively funded with financial or real assets. Assessment of the annuity approach as an alternative method for producing retirement income often occurs either within a life-cycle model context, where the goal (objective function) is to maximize the utility of consumption throughout the planning horizon, or within a shortfall probability context, where the annuity is deemed to represent a fail-safe instrument for generating threshold periodic income.

2. As benchmarks for assessing the historical performance of the retirement income portfolio or as cost-of-retirement benchmarks for determining the current portfolio's ability to support its income, gift, and bequest objectives.

3. As contracts available within a marketplace of investments that compete for the investor's dollar alongside mutual funds, exchange-traded funds, real assets, and so forth. Assessment of annuity solutions, in this context, requires knowledge of contract costs and provisions so that an investor can intelligently compare an annuity with other investment vehicles.[4]

Historical Return Approach: A Reliable Way to Model the Likelihood of Portfolio Depletion?

Perhaps the simplest approach for assessing a portfolio's ability to sustain retirement income is the historical return approach, which makes use of historical back testing (also known as rolling period analysis or overlapping period analysis). As the name implies, the historical return approach calculates the actual returns an investor's portfolio would have experienced given its asset allocation. Many retirement income risk models estimate the

---

[4]A forthcoming CFA Research Brief titled *Annuities and Retirement Income Planning* provides a more detailed discussion of the annuity market in the United States (Collins 2016).

likelihood of portfolio depletion by specifying a fixed withdrawal strategy throughout the planning horizon. Furthermore, the static withdrawal policy itself often operates over a fixed 20, 25, or 30 years. A commonly evaluated strategy is the 4% rule, which distributes annually, throughout retirement, an inflation-adjusted amount equal to 4% of the portfolio's initial dollar value.[5]

The historical back testing method tests the success or failure of the retirement plan for each unique planning horizon in the dataset of historical returns. The number of unique periods is typically determined by rolling up the start date of each planning horizon by a single increment of time. For example, Bierwirth (1994), often cited in articles offering financial planning advice, runs the analysis for the years 1926–1992 and uses a one-year rolling window to calculate 42 unique 27-year rolling periods. Each sample period is unique by virtue of the fact that its start year drops out of the dataset as a new ending year enters the dataset. Intervening years, however, continue to appear in multiple samples. Assuming that the past is indicative of the future, the historical model calculates the likelihood that a given level of retirement income is sustainable by dividing the number of successful planning periods by the total number of rolling periods for any given combination of asset allocation and retirement spending strategy. The combination with the highest success rate is considered optimal when measured by the likelihood that the unmodified—or autopilot—withdrawal strategy is sustainable over the applicable horizon. The acceptable retirement income sustainability rate is highly subjective and depends on investor circumstances and risk tolerance.[6]

Historical back testing is easy to understand and is a simple way to make relatively accurate assessments of what would have happened. An investor relying on such a methodology, however, should proceed with caution. This risk-modeling approach demands that an investor have faith in the highly dubious assumption that future returns will mimic realized past returns.[7] Although interesting, the pure history model fails to provide assurance that past conditions are sufficiently similar to current conditions that they act as guides to the future.

---

[5]This strategy is to withdraw 4% of a portfolio's initial value each year, with an adjustment for annual inflation. The result is a constant-dollar fixed retirement income stream. In essence, the investor self-annuitizes by creating a constant-dollar periodic cash flow income stream funded for as long as sufficient portfolio assets remain.

[6]See DiCarlo and Fast (2008) for a survey of opinions found in the financial advice literature regarding the acceptability of various levels of portfolio shortfall risk. The essay focuses primarily on standards of prudence for management of trust-owned investment portfolios.

[7]McGoun (1995) argues that the empirical distribution of financial asset price returns is not a measure of risk. It is merely a measure of historical realizations that may or may not be applicable to the current economic situation. McGoun presents a valuable history of risk measurement by economists.

Sustaining the Portfolio: Static Rules vs. Dynamic Portfolio Management

Some commentators favor following preset, bright-line rules adopted at the time of portfolio implementation. In practice, such rules are sometimes codified in a written investment policy statement. Under this static, or architectural, view of investment policy, sticking to preset asset management and withdrawal rules offers a high probability of achieving a safe and sustainable lifetime income.

Practitioners, however, have recently started to implement more dynamic systems engineering approaches to investment policy statements. This shift in emphasis, perhaps arising from the two severe equity market downturns in the first decade of this century, augments the importance of developing effective methods to monitor the ongoing financial health of the retirement portfolio.

Investors and advisers are becoming increasingly uncomfortable with portfolio management based on rule of thumb—that is, a useful but not necessarily reliable estimate—conventional wisdom. Paradoxically, however, some commentators respond to investment turbulence by replacing a single bright-line rule, such as a 4% withdrawal rate, with a veritable plethora of bright-line rules for all occasions. This literature review, however, only briefly touches on the myriad of suggested spending rules. Reliance on a single his-torical path of realized returns to develop and codify rules for asset allocation and distribution policy is, at the limit, an elaborate exercise in data mining.[8]

More often than not, an investor's retirement income preferences are suffi-ciently complex to call into question the value of standard modeling techniques that implement autopilot formulas, such as the 4% withdrawal rate rule. Rules-based portfolio management protocols often put the cart before the horse. Typically, actual retirement spending is governed by what the portfolio owner requires to fund the needs of the moment. Testing for portfolio failure rates or for the best asset allocation in the context of a monolithic withdrawal scheme is suboptimal if the objective is to develop financial planning recommendations. For normative research, the tools and techniques of retirement income portfolio evaluation should be sufficiently flexible to accommodate the inevitable changes in client goals and circumstances with which advisers and trustees must grapple.

This literature review demonstrates an evolution away from relatively simple retirement income risk models, which apply preset withdrawal rules to static asset allocations, toward models capable of capturing realistic and complicated dynamics of investor preferences and behaviors, economic shocks

---

[8]One type of data mining occurs when (1) a time-series analysis uncovers patterns or parame-ters that best fit the sample data and (2) the same data are used to develop and test the efficacy of asset management rules based on the patterns or parameters.

from various exogenous sources, and more credible trajectories of asset returns and inflation rates over a stochastic planning horizon. A credible assessment of portfolio sustainability requires ongoing monitoring of the resources available to discharge future cash flow liabilities.

Dynamic retirement income portfolio management encompasses a variety of strategies. Dynamic programming, for example, focuses on finding the optimal decision rules given well-defined investor preferences and constraints.[9] Fixed initial conditions (current resources) and well-specified control variables (jointly considering asset allocation and consumption strategies) often yield the Merton optimum in continuous-time finance models. The life-cycle model literature is an especially fruitful source for exploring how investors may optimize consumption and bequest objectives in the face of both deterministic and stochastic variables.

The investor should recognize, however, the limitation of any rules-based system derived from dynamic programming models. Different sequences of asset returns and inflation rates, liquidity demands, and other exogenous shocks may produce unacceptable results even when the optimal decision rules are followed. This possibility argues for simulation-based models that can solve path-dependent problems in which investor utility is a function of both the portfolio's value over time and the particular path taken to arrive at that value. Dynamic programming may not be appropriate when the investor faces multiple sources of complexity. Likewise, dynamic programming may not work well

---

[9]Dynamic programming is a mathematical theory of optimal sequential decisions under uncertainty. The Bellman principle of optimality governs the optimization process: Given an initial state and an initial strategy, the optimal strategy for the next period is the one that would be chosen if the analysis were to begin in the next period (i.e., the strategy for the next period must be optimal given the period-two set of conditions arising from the both the decisions made in the initial period and the value of period-two state variable[s]). The solution over a multiperiod horizon is a sequence of single-period optimization problems. The method examines various solution paths (control variables) until the end of the horizon; identifies the best decision-making rule(s) (the maximization or minimization of an objective function that is a mathematical expression of the investor's goal); and then traces the optimal path back to the beginning (determines the decision rule[s] for the control variables in each state by backward induction or other methods). The goal is to find a set of decision-making rules that are optimal irrespective of the specific conditions encountered in any single state (i.e., exogenous shocks to state variables do not change the decision rule[s] for control variables). Many life-cycle models seek to optimize investor utility (welfare) in terms of a spending control variable. Other commonly found control variables include asset allocation and retirement election (e.g., Social Security or pension benefit) dates. A variation of dynamic programming—optimal control—is commonly used to solve continuous time problems. Boundary control problems attempt to provide optimal decision rules given initial, ongoing, or terminal constraints (boundary conditions) on the objective function (i.e., at least $x of wealth must be available at the end of the stochastic planning horizon).

when confronted with sequences of investing and spending decisions where such decisions, reflecting time-dependent investor risk tolerance, create complex feedback loops.

Additionally, we find a variety of asset management strategies in the literature. For example, a portfolio insurance strategy makes discrete-time changes in asset weights in response to fluctuating portfolio values in order to replicate a convex option-like payoff structure. Investors may also consider both buy-and-hold (a static portfolio management approach) and constant-mix (a dynamic rebalancing approach) asset management strategies. Finally, we find a variety of empirical rules (adaptive portfolio withdrawal strategies) purporting to maximize the likelihood of portfolio sustainability. These rules are often recommended to investors because they would have produced successful results under previous market conditions. This is, of course, a variation on the historical back testing method for modeling retirement income portfolios. The key observation is that these portfolio management approaches require

- ongoing monitoring of the financial condition of the retirement income portfolio;

- careful consideration of the consequences of changes in wealth, spending requirements, and investor circumstances;

- identification and intelligent assessment of available asset management planning options; and

- an ability to quantify and articulate the probable economic consequences of implementing the specific investment options under consideration.

No investment risk model or asset management approach provides a magic bullet for prudent portfolio management. Longevity and portfolio sustainability models, on the one hand, and rules of thumb based on historical happenstance, on the other, are tools for producing financial insights; they are not substitutes for judgment.

Risk Measures, Benchmarks, and Portfolio Preferencing Metrics

In this literature review, we present a number of risk metrics that serve as portfolio preferencing criteria. These metrics include performance evaluation metrics (e.g., the Sharpe ratio, the information ratio, and Jensen's alpha measure). Another class of relevant metrics deals with shortfall risk: for example, shortfall probability relative to periodic income or terminal wealth targets, mean expected shortfall, and shortfall magnitude. In the worst case, the investor is concerned with portfolio depletion (i.e., bankruptcy) risk or, to use an alternate term, the "risk of ruin." Performance evaluation metrics help investors make inferences regarding *past* results. Shortfall risk metrics are *forward*-looking and generate probabilities based on either (1) the assumption that history repeats or (2) projections derived from an investment risk model. Early research sometimes incorporates questionable assumptions regarding the nature of asset prices and inflation, a flaw that can lead to unrealistic outputs. In contrast, much of recent research attempts to model the return-generating process more realistically.

This literature survey also reflects a shift in the nature and use of benchmarks. Early empirical studies use historical data as an implied benchmark against which to judge the prudence and suitability of asset management decisions.[10] At the same time, annuities feature prominently in actuarial journals; the payout from an annuity can serve as an alternative, forward-looking benchmark for retirement income. Of particular interest for this literature review is (1) the serious examination of the risks of financing retirement income through self-annuitization (i.e., maintaining a financial asset portfolio) versus the option to transfer risk to insurance carriers and (2) the optimality of an annuity-produced (and annuity-constrained) income stream. As financial economists became more familiar with actuarial research, the literature reflected an increased use of an annuity as a comparative benchmark.

Recent research moves beyond historical back testing and model-based shortfall projections to portfolio assessments based, in large part, on *current* observables: for example, the cost of lifetime income as revealed by the current price of an annuity. In turn, we see a new set of portfolio monitoring and evaluation metrics focused on retirement feasibility and portfolio solvency. Simplistically, if retirement assets earmarked for funding lifetime income are worth less than the current cost of an annuity, investors can *hope* that realized future returns are sufficiently favorable to overcome the current deficit. Hoping, however, puts a premium on ongoing performance monitoring lest the investor's hope lead the portfolio toward economic catastrophe.

The legal community has more than a passing interest in this discussion. Many irrevocable family trusts contain provisions directing the trustee to provide adequate lifetime income to the current beneficiary and to distribute terminal wealth to remainder beneficiaries. Trust language creates a dual set of claims against trust assets whenever the governing instrument directs the trustee to preserve either the nominal value or the inflation-adjusted value of initial assets for the remaindermen. The current beneficiary holds an income-based claim; the remaindermen hold a claim against terminal wealth. In such

---

[10]See, for example, Bengen (1994).

cases, trustees must impartially balance the competing claims of each beneficiary class. A failure to fulfill trustee duties may lead to allegations of a fiduciary breach, which, if upheld by a court, result in the payment of economic
damages from the trustee's personal assets. Just as the private investor needs
something more than hope, the prudent trustee must rely on something more
than good faith in the administration of the trust.

The stakes can be high in fiduciary breach litigation, and therefore, in the
early 1990s, the trust and estate section of the bar began an extensive discussion
of investment issues, trust distribution strategies, and portfolio sustainability
over the current beneficiary's lifetime. An important impetus for the discussion
was the 1994 adoption of the Uniform Prudent Investor Act by the National
Conference of Commissioners on Uniform State Laws. Usually, this discussion
is confined to legal journals and monographs that do not often appear as biblio-
graphical references in investment- and actuarial-oriented journals.[11]

Utility Maximization and Shortfall Minimization

Generally, one finds two types of retirement income models. Life-cycle models encompass a range of approaches in which investors use information to
make sequential decisions to try to attain their financial goals.[12] Although not
all life-cycle models are utility- (welfare-) maximizing models, most assume
that the investor tries to smooth lifetime spending (i.e., maintain a constant
marginal utility of consumption). Stochastic dynamic programing is a popular method for identifying asset management strategies that maximize aggregate utility over the investor's lifetime.[13]

In contrast, shortfall minimization models often test autopilot asset allocations and spending rules. Historical backtests, bootstrapped reshuffling of
historical returns, and Monte Carlo simulations of pre-parameterized distributions are popular methods of assessing the likelihood of a shortfall should a
myopic investor elect to stay the course throughout all economic conditions.[14]

In some cases, shortfall minimization leads to allocations and withdrawal
strategies that differ substantially from those recommended by life-cycle

---

[11]See, for example, Collins, Savage, and Stampfli (2000).

[12]A good review of the history of life-cycle models is found in Browning and Crossley (2001).

[13]When variables evolve continuously—a diffusion—they are modeled as a continuous-time
stochastic process.

[14]This set of metrics includes a variety of risk measures, including the likelihood of a shortfall
in either periodic consumption or terminal wealth; an unacceptable variance in periodic consumption; the expected value of a shortfall, either in terms of the present value of a shortfall
or in terms of the mean expected shortfall given that a shortfall occurs; the magnitude or
duration (time without funds) of a shortfall; a distribution of shortfall results, and so forth.
Bajtelsmit, Rappaport, and Foster (2013) provide a helpful review of shortfall risk metrics.

models that purport to optimize investor utility.[15] An important research advance occurred in the mid-2000s, when several authors asked whether it is possible to reconcile the two types of retirement income risk models.[16] Generally speaking, a condition for resolution occurs when one of the following happens:

- The utility function being optimized in life-cycle models shifts away from constant relative risk aversion (CRRA), where risk aversion is invariant to changes in the level of wealth, to either hyperbolic absolute risk aversion (HARA), where risk aversion (decreasing or increasing) is a possibly linear function of the wealth level, or to a form of state-preference utility in which asset payoffs in one economic (or health) state are preferred to equivalent or greater payoffs in other states. Aggregate utility calculated by applying a homogenous utility function over every economic state (i.e., across a distribution of possible investment results) gives way to subjective preferences that differ across each state (i.e., state-contingent preferences). In prosperous states, the investor may exhibit a "keep up with the Joneses" (i.e., a desire to compete in terms of wealth/goods with others in the community) utility function; in poor states, the investor may exhibit an "avoid the soup kitchen" utility function. The main point is that the utility function may manifest different shapes as the investor's economic and personal circumstances change: The function is no longer homogenous.

- A minimum threshold level of income or wealth is introduced into the model. The presence of such a consumption floor means that the investor derives utility only for amounts equal to or in excess of the target income or wealth level.

The importance of reconciling shortfall risk–minimization approaches and utility-maximization approaches to investment and spending decisions cannot be overstated. This line of research also motivates (1) a reassessment of the role of annuities as a wealth management tool and (2) the use of an annuity-based

---

[15]This topic is the primary focus of Harlow and Brown (2014).

[16]Although this literature review deals with retirement income models, there is a long academic history of model building using various combinations of utility functions. A good early survey is found in Fishburn (1977). Traditional von Neumann and Morgenstern utility-based models are sometimes combined with models derived from behavioral finance research (e.g., Diecidue and Van De Ven [2008]), or with models incorporating safety-first utility (e.g., Levy and Levy [2009]). These articles are cited later in this literature review. Although outside the direct scope of retirement income modeling, the development of mathematical expressions that combine shortfall probability avoidance preferences, behavioral insights into loss aversion and prospect theory, safety-first criteria, and utility-based decision models provides an interesting perspective into the theory of portfolio choice. These topics are explored in greater detail in Collins, Lam, and Stampfli (2015b).

benchmark to compare investment strategies. Furthermore, it provides intellectual underpinning for assessing the financial health of a retirement income portfolio in terms of solvency and feasibility metrics, and it opens portfolio monitoring to a richer set of risk metrics extending well beyond projections of the likelihood of failure.

Assessing the Retirement Income Portfolio: Solvency vs. Shortfall

Sustainability of adequate income over a lifetime is a critical portfolio objective for retired investors. Commentators often define sustainability in terms of (1) a portfolio's ability to continue to make distributions throughout the applicable planning horizon or (2) a portfolio's ability to fund a minimum level of target income at every interval during the planning horizon. The first approach focuses on the likelihood of ending with positive wealth or, if wealth is depleted prior to the end of the planning horizon, on the magnitude and duration of the shortfall; the second focuses on the likelihood of consistently meeting all period-by-period minimum cash flow requirements.

Risk models help advisers assess a portfolio's ability to provide adequate cash flow throughout retirement. Conclusions about cash flow sustainability are usually reached by determining the likelihood that withdrawals (fixed amounts, percentage of corpus, or dynamic) can be maintained for either deterministic or stochastic time periods under various asset allocations and longevity assumptions. It is the risk model that generates the distribution of future results, and therefore, probability assessments are not independent of the model.[17]

A critical distinction must be drawn between *sustainability*—the probability, calculated by the risk model, that future financial market returns are sufficient to defease targeted cash flows—and *feasibility*, a judgment regarding the current ability of the portfolio to fund the present value of required cash flows. The feasibility condition requires that the current market value of assets equals the stochastic present value of the lifetime target income plus, if relevant, gifts and bequests.[18] Conceptually, it is useful to consider portfolio monitoring as a test of a portfolio's funded status (i.e., as an activity occurring within the context of "free boundary" problems, a familiar concept in mathematics and physics).

---

[17]Maurer, Albrecht, and Ruckpaul (2001) provide a detailed assessment of shortfall risk measures. They conclude that ". . .the use of the shortfall probability alone is insufficient for the assessment of the risk of stock investments in the long run. . . . The probability of a loss or a shortfall decreases with the length of the time horizon. However, the average level of the loss or the shortfall respectively, given a loss or a shortfall has occurred, increases" (p. 488).
[18]We are grateful to Laurence Siegel for pointing out that "feasibility" is best understood as full funding and "sustainability" as a p-value.

One class of free boundary problems, known as Stefan problems, involves estimating the demarcation between two regions where the line of demarcation is not fixed.[19] A classic example is estimating the location of the boundary between solid ice and liquid water when the temperature drops below freezing. In winter, the depth of a Minnesota lake's boundary between ice and water fluctuates according to the random variable of water temperature. In cold weather, the ice pack is thick; in warmer weather, it thins.

By analogy, when assessing a retirement income portfolio in terms of the feasibility condition, the investor needs to determine the line of demarcation between two regions—a region of wealth surplus, in which the portfolio's current value is able to support financial objectives, and a region of wealth deficit, in which the portfolio's current value is not able to support financial objectives. A bull market tends to move a portfolio further into the feasible region—the region of wealth surplus. A bear market, however, tends to move it toward the infeasible region. If the portfolio is initially feasible, a bear market moves it toward the free boundary that separates the regions. As wealth depletion pushes the portfolio further and further toward the region of infeasibility, the consequences of investor actions or inactions are magnified in the sense that an ill-considered asset management decision may generate not merely losses but losses from which the portfolio can never recover. The investor has to know, in effect, the thickness of the ice pack, lest undue optimism induce her to conduct her financial affairs on thin ice.

This literature review presents the intellectual background for considering management of a retirement income portfolio as a free boundary problem. In many respects, the research history expresses the retirement planning solution in terms of a utility-based model in which the boundary is defined either in option valuation terms (e.g., optimal time to annuitize) or as a boundary control problem in which wealth is not allowed to drop below the stochastic present value of liabilities, a periodic consumption level, a utility value, or some other similarly defined demarcation level.

The contribution of legal commentary to this discussion is its focus on the economic consequences of portfolio management decisions in terms of the legitimate economic expectations of interested parties where such expectations

---

[19]See Friedman (2000). Free boundary problems require solutions to differential equations. An introduction to these equations within the context of trust portfolio management is provided by Collins and Stampfli (2001). A partial differential equation is an equation that reflects the simultaneous rates of change of several independent variables. Not all partial differential equations have a closed-form (analytical) solution. When risk modeling demands (1) considering various decision points over time, (2) incorporating uncertainty from various sources, or (3) using complex systems of independent variables, numerical methods are required to approximate a solution.

are couched in terms of terminal dollar wealth and ongoing income levels. The contribution of the actuarial literature is the analysis of annuity solutions to the portfolio sustainability problem. The insights derived from this branch of intellectual study enable researchers to redefine the retirement income problem in terms of annuity pricing formulas that calculate the present-day cost of providing future periodic income.

This literature review uses the term "free boundary" in several contexts: (1) as an element in a barrier control problem, (2) as an accounting concept—the current value of assets minus the stochastic present value of liabilities, (3) as a benchmark-relative measure (i.e., the value of assets compared with an annuity-cost benchmark), (4) as a solution point for a differential equation in the classic mathematical definition of free boundary problems, and (5) as a reference point for both prior research and ongoing research in the field of retirement income portfolio monitoring and evaluation. Benchmarking the retirement income portfolio in terms of an objective, market-determined cost benchmark enables researchers to create models that define a free boundary as the point where a portfolio becomes technically insolvent because it violates the feasibility condition—that is, assets are less than liabilities. Specifically, absent bequest objectives, the free boundary lies at the point where the current market value of assets is less than the current cost of a single-premium annuity priced to provide a minimum acceptable lifetime income. Several recent retirement income models express longevity risk in terms of annuity cost. Longevity risk reduces to a dollar value!

Monitoring the feasibility condition differs from assessing a portfolio's financial health in terms of the likelihood of sustainability over the planning horizon. As noted, the likelihood of future portfolio depletion often expresses a shortfall probability derived from projections made by risk models using Monte Carlo simulation or bootstrap analysis. Unlike the feasibility condition, which is a function of current market observables, the shortfall probability metric is the risk model's best guess. Depending on the projected time of portfolio depletion, the risk to the investor may be severe if other assets (e.g., Social Security, home equity, family support) cannot cushion the magnitude and duration of the shortfall. However, advances in modeling facilitate prudent portfolio surveillance and monitoring by tracking both shortfall and feasibility risk metrics. Over time, the locus of action in retirement income planning shifts from a search for the best portfolio design and spending rules to dynamic portfolio monitoring and intelligent assessment of asset management decisions.[20]

---

[20]This topic is the focus of Collins et al. (2015b).

Part One: Retirement Income Risk Models (1965–2005)

Setting the Stage: Optimizing Retirement Consumption/ Minimizing Shortfall Probability

Many academic commentaries trace their origin to Yaari (1965), who demonstrates that investors without a bequest objective and with access to actuarially fair annuities in a complete market setting—one where insurance or financial instruments span *all economic risks* faced by the investor—will hold all wealth in "actuarial notes" (p. 140). Yaari considers how the investor can optimize discounted expected utility over both a deterministic period and an uncertain lifespan where the investor places a value on both consumption and bequests. Investors lacking a bequest objective will maximize a utility function for consumption only, and their challenge is to find the optimal feasible consumption plan when the planning horizon is uncertain. Under the Yaari complete market model, annuities put the investor on the optimal feasible consumption path.

When a bequest motive exists, however, the investor must solve for optimization of two decision variables: a feasible consumption plan and a feasible savings plan. Assuming no labor income, consumption is funded entirely with annuities, whereas the savings plan's asset allocation is a function of available investment returns. In equilibrium, the marginal utility of the consumption plan will exactly equal that of the saving plan. Yaari makes the important observation that when annuities are available, ". . .the consumer can separate the consumption decision from the bequest decision" (p. 149). In the absence of annuities, such a separation is not possible. Later studies are building on Yaari's observations whenever their authors recommend a two-fund solution (a guaranteed annuity income plus investment of surplus wealth in a performance-seeking portfolio) to the retirement income/bequest challenge.

Yaari's classic paper is also an important source document for researchers applying a portfolio shortfall probability risk metric: "The chance-constrained programming approach requires that the constraint (in this case the wealth constraint) be met with probability λ or more, where λ is some number fixed in advance, say 0.95" (p. 139).

Under this evaluation metric, the optimal portfolio minimizes shortfall probability. However, Yaari does not develop a probability-of-success approach to evaluating portfolio choice. Rather, he evaluates investment and actuarial solutions in terms of maximizing investor utility (welfare) over the applicable planning horizon at an appropriate discount rate for a risk-averse investor manifesting a possibly time-varying preference for consumption as a function of age. Yaari's model sets the table for future inquiry in that it acknowledges (1) the usefulness of both utility-based life-cycle modeling and shortfall risk modeling, (2) the existence of both actuarial- and investment-oriented solutions, and (3) the importance of the consumer's preference function ("impatience") with respect to the timing and magnitude of retirement spending.

Milevsky, Ho, and Robinson (1997) highlight the significance of shortfall probability as a preferencing criterion for a retirement income investment strategy. They frame the optimization problem in terms of projecting the time when a portfolio, maintaining a fixed vector of asset allocation weights and earning a stochastic return, suffers depletion under the stress of spending requirements. The optimal asset allocation is the one that depletes the portfolio at the latest feasible future date.

Milevsky et al. (1997) decompose wealth into asset and liability components: Net portfolio value at any future date consists of the compound growth of initial wealth less the income payout liability defined as the accumulated value of an annuity due. The date of ruin—the "conditional first time exit"— is the limit of time for which wealth is greater than consumption demands. Beyond this time, the investor will run out of money.

Additionally, Milevsky et al. (1997) are some of the first to argue for the need for dynamic asset allocation in the face of a static spending policy— especially where there is a lower boundary designating an acceptable spending level. The study is an early example of the use of annuity pricing factors to value retirement liabilities. Although the authors are primarily interested in solving for the date of financial ruin, their method is generally conformable to a free boundary approach. The existence of a threshold, or minimum, periodic income need throughout each retirement period becomes an increasingly important aspect of risk modeling in future studies.

Milevsky published a follow-on study in 1998 that presents and explores the importance of the wealth/consumption ratio in identifying the optimal asset allocation. He introduces the topic of the optimal time to exercise an option to annuitize financial wealth, which he expresses in option valuation terms. A threshold condition for annuitization occurs when annuity mortality credits overtake annuity costs. The recommended course is to evaluate the portfolio after each period. If there is surplus wealth (i.e., the portfolio's current market value is greater than the present value of projected future spending), then it is beneficial to delay exercise of the annuitization option. A primary justification for delay is that early exercise destroys the option's time value; all else being equal, the cost of an annuity-provided income stream should decrease as the investor ages. Note that delay is not risk free because the annuity's future costs may rise as a function of interest rate changes. The strategy of delaying for as long as possible, however, implies that prudent portfolio management does not allow financial wealth to drop below the present value of consumption. An individual is better off deferring purchase of an annuity if his after-consumption wealth at the beginning of period x is greater than the annuity's cost at the beginning of period $x + 1$.[21]

Because the purchase of an annuity is an irrevocable decision to pay a non-refundable sum to an insurance company and because the decision eliminates liquidity and the ability to make bequests, the investor should defer annuitization, according to Milevsky (1998), for as long as possible, provided that the risk of failing to acquire an adequate lifetime income stream remains within tolerable levels. Later studies by Milevsky and others (e.g., Milevsky and Young 2007), de-emphasize the importance of the wealth/consumption ratio in favor of a pure option-to-annuitize valuation approach. These researchers argue that holding investments in a risky-asset portfolio beyond the optimal stopping time could result in further deterioration in portfolio values to the detriment of the investor. Milevsky's shifting approaches might, at first read, seem contradictory because they lead to seemingly different conclusions regarding preferred portfolio management decisions. The apparent contradiction, however, is more the byproduct of differing mathematical explorations of decision-making approaches than the result of inconsistent thinking.

Dybvig (1999) is one of the first to explore the link between asset allocation policy and portfolio spending policy.[22] He argues that asset allocation and spending decisions must be made jointly. Common practice is to link spending to the long-term expected return of the strategic asset allocation—a static linkage that does not provide dynamic feedback to the investor. Dybvig, like Milevsky, advocates a sequential (year-by-year) decision-making process. Asset allocation changes dynamically to reflect changes in the value of wealth, interest rates, and spending objectives. Both Dybvig (1999) and Milevsky (1998) emphasize the importance of (1) monitoring and (2) periodically evaluating asset management decisions. As such, they are important in the justification of active management of the retirement income portfolio.[23]

---

[21]This raises the question of how an investor projects the annuity's cost in period $x + 1$. The distribution of the future cost of annuity contracts assumes increasing importance in future research.

[22]Although Dybvig (1999) addresses perpetual (e.g., educational) endowments, his conclusions can be transferred to limited-life endowments, such as an investor's retirement savings.

[23]We distinguish between active *investing*, which is the attempt to beat the market through stock selection and market timing, and active *management*, which requires ongoing portfolio monitoring and review. Even a portfolio consisting entirely of index funds often requires the investor's active involvement for rebalancing, asset allocation changes, spending decisions, and so forth.

Investment vs. Actuarial Solutions

Several papers published during this period explore the question of whether annuitization, especially in periods of low interest rates, provides either an optimal income stream or a preferred portfolio management strategy. For example, Mitchell, Poterba, Warshawsky, and Brown (1999) note that annuities are bond-backed portfolios acquired by insurance companies operating in the capital markets. Whereas the duration of an annuity is, in general, greater than the duration of an underlying bond portfolio, an investor who buys a nominal dollar annuity exchanges systematic longevity risk for systematic purchasing power risk. Albrecht and Maurer (2001) conclude that annuities purchased in low interest rate environments produce modest payouts that, in most cases, can be achieved through self-annuitization of a risky asset portfolio. At older ages and in higher interest rate environments, however, attempting to match an annuity payout with distributions from a risky-asset portfolio runs a much higher risk of ruin.

These observations have implications for investors in low interest rate environments. Brown, Mitchell, and Poterba (2001) point out that maintaining the constant-dollar value of consumption may not be the optimal consumption path. Smoothed consumption is the ability to keep the marginal utility—as opposed to the dollar value—of expenditures steady. Constant (real) annuity income may not reflect the time preferences of retired investors. Interestingly, Brown (2001) himself suggests a possible solution. If there is sufficient surplus wealth, the investor may wish to annuitize most wealth so that there is a choice to spend most or all of the periodic payment if the time-preference discount rate is high or to save and reinvest a portion of each payment if the time-preference discount rate is low. Brown's observations suggest that annuitization might be considered even when current wealth is well above the free boundary location. Part Three of this literature review provides additional discussion on this topic.

In a paper presented at the Third Annual Conference of the Retirement Research Consortium, Poterba (2001) links the topic of the optimal retirement income stream with the concept of option-based optimal stopping time for annuitization. Optimal stopping time approaches to asset management decision making (i.e., the optimal time to switch from a risky-asset portfolio to annuity-generated income) constitute an important alternative to the free boundary approach. Poterba notes that annuitizing all wealth at a single moment (an "optimal stopping time") may not, in fact, be optimal. It is, in his opinion, a type of annuity market timing. Poterba develops the theme of "time diversification" of annuity purchases. Variation in bond returns generates a substantial variation in annuity payout rates over time; therefore, annuitizing all wealth at a single moment is a risky strategy.

The literature reveals an ongoing tension among commentators on the subject of optimal annuity timing. Some suggest that investors should annuitize all wealth at the point in time when the annuity contract's mortality premium exceeds the expected premium from holding a risky asset portfolio—an option valuation approach that stresses the fact that annuities are a cost-efficient way to generate income. Others suggest that investors should annuitize all wealth as soon as they can lock in their desired future income stream. Finally, others suggest that, if prudent, investors should delay exercising the option to annuitize. The recommendation to delay stems from the observations that (1) immediate annuitization may impose an unacceptable constraint on future consumption and (2) investors value smoothed marginal utility of lifetime consumption more than a fixed periodic dollar-value income.

This ongoing debate is illuminated by Milevsky and Huang (2011). The authors echo Poterba's (2001) arguments regarding the optimality of securing retirement income by annuitizing all wealth at a single moment. However, they make their case within the context of maximizing utility of consumption: "The utility-maximizing retiree is not willing to reduce their initial standard of living simply because of a small probability they will reach age 105. . . . They deal with longevity risk by setting aside a financial reserve and by planning to reduce consumption if that risk materializes in proportion to the survival probability and linked to their risk aversion" (p. 48). The authors quote Irving Fisher (1930): ". . . [the investor] has a high degree of impatience for income, because he expects to die, and he thinks, 'Why shouldn't I enjoy myself during the few years that remain instead of piling up for the remote future?'" (Milevsky and Huang 2011, p. 388).

We expand the discussion of the Fisher view of utility maximization in Part Three when we examine more closely the calculation of an annuity's utility value under life-cycle models of consumption. Part Three also charts the impact of more complex life-cycle retirement risk models that incorporate other utility functions, such as Epstein–Zin preferences,[24] state preference theory, and habit persistence.[25]

---

[24]Epstein–Zin utility is discussed in greater detail in the Part Two section "Utility—Again."

[25]Yaari acknowledges the importance of Fisher utility and includes a term for the investor's subjective discount rate (impatience) that may differ from the prevailing risk-free rate. Consumption is decreasing ". . .whenever the rate of subjective discount is greater than the rate of interest." (p. 138) Yaari, however, laments that research models incorporate a number of simplifying assumptions (". . .one makes assumptions to suit the problem at hand. . .") (p. 137); and that the form of his model's utility function means ". . .that the consumer's preferences are independent over time. This is not a very happy assumption, but unfortunately some strong assumption of this sort must be made in order to make the problem manageable." (p. 137). It is not too far off the mark to assert that future research studies either seek to address and overcome such limitations or simply ignore them.

It is interesting to contrast Poterba's (2001) view with that expressed by Ameriks and Yakoboski (2003): "There is an inherent tradeoff between maintaining a stock of assets and supporting a flow of income" (p. 18). The annuity contract, according to Ameriks and Yakoboski, is valuable insofar as it allows retirees to achieve the greatest efficiency in spending money throughout retirement. Provided that annuity contract costs are reasonable, the authors point out that annuitization produces a dollar of lifetime income for older-age investors at a cheaper cost than any other investment alternative. The debate between annuitization and self-annuitization takes center stage during this period. Recommendations concerning the optimal time to exercise an annuitization option reflect either the cost-efficiency school of thought (e.g., mortality credits dominate the expected risky asset portfolio premium) or the utility maximization school of thought (e.g., a dynamic programming approach to the retirement consumption objective).

Orszag (2002a) contributes to the cost-efficiency school of thought by taking an option valuation approach; the optimal time to annuitize is the point when the annuity produces an income stream higher than a portfolio drawdown program. Thus, it is the ratio of consumption from the portfolio to consumption from the annuity that determines the optimal time for annuitization—not the wealth-to-consumption ratio. Although annuity mortality credits are larger at older ages, Orszag generally recommends a top-down approach in which annuitization is delayed until an optimal stopping time. However, in a nod to the merits of utility-based arguments, he notes that annuities lock in the budget constraint, meaning that there is a risk of losing potentially higher income at later ages if annuitization occurs too early in retirement.

Kapur and Orszag (2002) together develop further the concept of the annuity premium—that is, the spread between annuity yields and long-term government bond yields. Capturing this spread requires "capital sacrifice" (p. 2). Thus, a decision to acquire an immediate payout annuity to protect the current standard of living involves defending capital sacrifice. The annuity premium crowds out bonds from the portfolio.[26] If, however, equity is used to purchase an annuity, the decision is to exchange the expected equity risk premium for the annuity premium. Kapur and Orszag contend that whenever the annuity premium exceeds the expected equity risk premium, the option to annuitize should be exercised. This is a preference-free

---

[26]An annuity pays bond interest plus an extra amount to contract holders for as long as they live. Ultimately, the bond defaults and fails to return principal, but this event occurs only at the annuitant's death. The default is, in fact, the source of the extra amount—the annuity premium—enjoyed by all annuitants participating in the mortality-pooling arrangement.

calculation—a question of stochastic dominance rather than investor utility or target income feasibility.

However, perhaps in an effort to bridge the two approaches to the retirement consumption problem, Orszag (2002b) presents a third essay in which he reintroduces a preferencing criterion by establishing a lower bound consumption target. The consequences of introducing a threshold, lower-income boundary into the model are profound.[27] Orszag solves a differential equation to determine the income withdrawal rate target that is the reciprocal of the consumption target. The withdrawal rate calculation, however, ignores the influence of stochastic mortality. Orszag defines it as the rate that will drive the portfolio value to zero after x number of years, where x is a fixed number.

Orszag (2002b), in contrast to Poterba (2001), argues that annuities are more attractive than bonds in low interest rate environments because the annuity mortality premium becomes a greater percentage of total current income. Orszag's view also contrasts, for example, with that of Chen and Milevsky (2003). They point out that payouts on annuities are a function of the prevailing interest rate at the time the contract is executed. As a consequence, "locking in a fixed annuity is implicitly a market-timing play" (p. 4).

Stabile (2006) defines a region where it is not optimal to annuitize as well as a region where the investor immediately annuitizes all wealth. The regions are separated by a boundary that is defined by a utility of wealth value function, rather than by a dollar-denominated free boundary. The optimal time for annuitization occurs when the dynamic programming solution to the value function indicates that investor preferences are best served through an actuarial—as opposed to an investment-oriented—solution. If the investor's utility-adjusted wealth remains above the lower threshold, then the investment program continues (i.e., annuitization is deferred). His risk model indicates that, if wealth remains greater than a threshold amount, the investor continues to participate in financial markets, even when the investor's risk aversion for income derived in financial markets is higher than that for annuity payouts. If the investor approaches the boundary from below, however, the decision rule is to purchase an annuity at the boundary. If the investor does not immediately annuitize at the boundary, the situation might deteriorate further.

Gerrard, Haberman, and Vigna (2004) provide an interesting variation of the boundary problem and a counterpoint to Stabile's (2006) observations. They point out that the region of annuitization might occur either at a

---

[27]The implications of sustaining a threshold income form a major topic in Part Three of this literature survey.

minimum boundary to protect against further deterioration of wealth or at a maximum boundary, which is defined as the fund size sufficient to purchase a large lifetime income stream. If the annuitization benefit is sufficiently large, there is little need to continue investing in a risky asset portfolio; the utility of the extra cash generated by investing grows vanishingly small.

The authors' model incorporates a quadratic loss (disutility) function when the investment portfolio fails to maintain an amount sufficient to purchase a single premium immediate annuity (SPIA) for the investor's target income. The lower an investor's risk aversion, the higher the future income target that the financial asset portfolio must fund. Interestingly, a utility penalty is assigned both when the investment portfolio underperforms its target and when it outperforms. Underperformance indicates that the desired standard of living is at risk; outperformance indicates that the portfolio could have generated the required return with less risk. The authors estimate optimal asset management strategies for both a constant income target and an exponentially increasing income target. Given the model's assumptions regarding quadratic risk aversion, it is not surprising that the optimal solution is the Merton optimum adjusted for the investor's risk aversion with respect to income and bequest goals.

The Gerrard et al. (2004) study is an early example of a series of works focusing on the cost of retirement. Some commentators argue that, absent a bequest motive, unspent funds represent a missed opportunity to improve lifetime living standards; others argue that overfunding retirement income targets misaligns financial goals (liabilities) with the assets designed to fund them. See, for example, Scott, Sharpe, and Watson (2009), who assert that a truly risk-free retirement consumption strategy never exhibits either a surplus or deficit. Under this view, any strategy that matches constant spending with volatile (uncertain) return outcomes is suboptimal in several respects: (1) There is a positive probability of ruin, and (2) there is a cost to generate an unneeded or low-utility surplus.

Milevsky reappears in our survey of academic literature. Milevsky, Moore, and Young (2004) employ a barrier control problem approach to the issue. When current wealth is greater than the market price of a target annuity income stream, the investor will annuitize to lock in the targeted lifetime consumption. However, when wealth is insufficient, the issue becomes the optimal time to buy the annuity: "The optimal annuity-purchasing scheme is a type of barrier control" (p. 12). To the left of the barrier—wealth is below the stochastic present value of consumption—the investor makes no annuity purchase; to the right of the barrier, the investor will buy an annuity sufficient to guarantee the targeted periodic income.

Moving beyond the Constant Relative Risk Aversion Assumption: A Minimum Income Need

Vanduffel, Dhaene, Goovaerts, and Kaas (2003) explore the topic of how much money (reserves) an insurance company needs in order to ensure funding adequacy for a stream of future liability payments at a given confidence level. Although their primary intended audience is insurance company actuaries, the authors develop a portfolio management approach that forms a solid basis for ascertaining portfolio sustainability and for implementing procedures to protect the portfolio's ability to provide required future payments.

To meet payment obligations with certainty, the authors argue, the replicating portfolio must consist of *n* zero-coupon bonds, assuming that the liability is deterministic. They also calculate, however, the optimal reserve when the investment portfolio generates stochastic, rather than certain returns. In this case, the objective is to determine the reserve, or provision "such that the probability that we will be able to meet our future obligations will be sufficiently large. Conversely, if the level of the provision is given, our methodology will enable us to compute the probability that we will be able to meet our future obligations under the given investment strategy" (p. 405). When the level of the provision or reserve is given, as in the case of a retirement income portfolio, "the optimal investment strategy could be determined as the one leading to the maximal probability that we will be able to meet our future obligations" (p. 406).[28]

Vanduffel et al. (2003) detail how to calculate the provision when the future payments are known and when the provision is invested in a stochastic return process. Given a stream of liability payments, the provision must have a value equal to or greater than zero at the end of the applicable planning horizon. The reserve is adequate if its level is greater than the stochastic present value (PV) of the payments to be made. The liability is deterministic, but the PV of the liability payment stream is subject to changes in the discount rate. Therefore, the PV of the liability is also stochastic.

A limitation of defining the optimal reserve in terms of "reaching the finish" (Vanduffel et al. 2003, p. 407) is that there may be situations in which the interim value of the reserve falls below a threshold level, a condition that may violate regulatory requirements or otherwise be undesirable. The problem

---

[28]The reader will recognize this as a variation on the "chance-constrained programming approach" introduced—but not developed—in Yaari (1965). A more recent variation on the hurdle race approach to asset management is Scott (2008), who suggests that the initial provision might be relatively small if the investor is willing to purchase a deferred annuity—that is, a contingent payout life annuity that provides a periodic income only to contract holders who survive to an advanced age.

23

becomes one of calculating the optimal reserve not only in terms of the ultimate goal but also in terms of the period-to-period reserve value: "The conditions that year-to-year the provision R_j is larger than a given deterministic value V_j with a sufficiently large probability. These additional requirements are the 'hurdles' that have to be taken" (p. 407). The authors' approach shares many similarities with a free boundary framework for prudent asset management, particularly with respect to meeting interim "hurdles" or solvency checkpoints as part of monitoring the retirement feasibility condition.

We can draw a direct line from Yaari (1965) to Blake, Cairns, and Dowd (2003). Yaari, as noted, opts to use a utility-of-consumption approach for determining the optimal consumption path for investors with limited resources and no bequest objective. However, in order to achieve mathematical tractability, Yaari, as well as most commentators following in his footsteps, assumes that the risk aversion function remains constant despite changes in the level of wealth.

Although it had long been recognized that constant relative risk aversion applies to investors only under a limited number of conditions,[29] through the end of the 20th century, many studies nevertheless evaluate mathematical models based on the twin assumptions of lognormal risky-asset return distributions (a geometric Brownian process) and constant relative risk aversion on the part of investors. These assumptions have profound consequences. If return distributions are similar to the bell curve, then a sequence of below-the-mean returns is merely a series of unlucky draws from a stable distribution. Realized results carry little information regarding the desirability of holding the risky-asset portfolio in future periods, and changes in investment strategy may be unwarranted because the nature of the underlying distribution (i.e., the probability of future sequences of positive or negative returns) remains unchanged. Likewise, the assumption of constant relative risk aversion assumes that an investor maintains full willingness to continue a risky venture despite the pressure on current surplus—resources above the free boundary line. Operating together, these twin assumptions provide a powerful rationale for staying the course, trusting in the restorative power of capital markets, and maintaining equanimity in the face of decreasing wealth.

Blake et al. (2003), by contrast, restore the focus to the wealth/consumption ratio. They argue that optimal annuitization is a function of investment performance *and* the size of the wealth fund. Smaller-sized accounts produce less income, and the marginal utility of the excess income from annuitization has greater value: "The marginal utility of consumption gets large as the fund size gets small" (p. 43). The annuitization trigger changes from an optimal stopping time problem—annuitize when the annuity mortality premium exceeds the

---

[29]For a helpful discussion, see Venter (1983).

expected equity risk premium—to a decision directly tied to portfolio size relative to spending demands: "A larger fund size makes it more likely that the plan member will delay annuitization" (p. 45). This important study is one of the first to model several different utility functions to ascertain how output changes with changes in the utility function's form.

We also refer readers to Davidoff, Brown, and Diamond (2003) regarding the economic assumption of complete markets—an assumption that starts with Yaari (1965) and continues throughout the history of academic commentary. Davidoff et al. relax Yaari's complete market assumption and demonstrate that, absent a bequest motive, investors will annuitize some wealth as long as annuities pay a higher return than assets of comparable risk.

Utility Maximization and Shortfall Probability Minimization

By 2005, several research paths found an elegant synthesis in Abbas and Matheson (2005). The importance of this paper rests, in part, in the authors' observation that utility-based decision making is compatible with shortfall- or target-based decision theory in the presence of a required minimum level of income that must be maintained throughout the applicable planning horizon.

Classical utility theory states that investors seek to optimize utility over the distribution of potential outcomes. However, the presence of a lower bound creates a type of "step-utility function" (Abbas and Matheson 2005, p. 373) that divides outcomes into two regions—acceptable and unacceptable.[30] With suitable mathematical transforms, the utility of the investment project is equal to the probability that the result is above an "aspiration level" that divides the two regions (p. 377). Although the aspiration level is the boundary between satisfactory and unsatisfactory, its location constantly changes because of "changes in the lottery that the individual is facing" (p. 377).

For investment issues, the aspiration level changes with such factors as wealth level and liability values. Probability distributions may, however, change through time, and the targets may have to be revised to reflect updated information: "Pursuing a fixed goal may be operationally motivational when things are going smoothly, but when major impacts, such as setbacks or new opportunities, create a need to re-evaluate alternatives, the normative approach demands determining new targets. . . . Simply maximizing the probability of reaching the old target is no longer optimal" (p. 384).

The authors provide solid underpinning for asserting the importance of active monitoring and portfolio surveillance in terms of the investor's retirement income goals. We also note that Stutzer (2003) discusses differences

---

[30]The utility function, at the point where it reaches the aspiration level, is found to exhibit a discontinuity in other research. See, for example, Diecidue and Van De Ven (2008).

between the classical approach of portfolio optimization based on utility maximization and approaches based on shortfall probability minimization.[31]

Both Abbas and Matheson (2005) and Stutzer (2003) argue that the presence of a consumption floor—a lower boundary based on a required periodic income stream—changes the nature of the decision-making process. Kingston and Thorp (2005) further advance this argument and, in doing so, clarify the relationship between investor utility (welfare) and portfolio management decisions. They advance a rationale for a bottom-up approach to annuitization (i.e., annuitize as soon as possible) similar to the one made several years later by Babbel and Merrill (2007). The minimum standard of living target is fully funded ("escrowed") by the annuity. The risk-averse investor secures this floor income as soon as possible and, therefore, tends to favor early exercise of the option to annuitize.[32]

Babbel and Merrill (2007), however, also offer a discussion about the reasons for and merits of delaying annuitization: Because risky assets carry the expectation of high return, a longer period of holding such assets "offers people a chance to improve their budget constraint that evaporates after annuitization. So even risk-averse individuals may decide to delay in the expectation of creating more wealth and enjoying a higher long-term income" (p. 226). Individuals who (subjectively) anticipate a long lifespan may delay annuitization given the potential benefits of (1) lower future annuity costs, especially if interest rates increase, and (2) higher returns from exposure to risky assets.

Given the fact that an annuity purchase decision is irreversible and that the real option to annuitize has time value, the Kingston–Thorp (2005) analysis parallels the Milevsky–Moore–Young (2004) assertion that an investor will delay annuitization until the expected return from the annuity contract exceeds that of other financial instruments exhibiting comparable risk. In contrast to the Milevsky–Moore–Young model, which assumes CRRA, Kingston and Thorp assume HARA, which is a function suggesting that an investor gains utility only for consumption in excess of either a static or fixed floor or, for investors who ratchet up their spending targets, for consumption in excess of a dynamically changing floor. The Kingston–Thorp model assumes that the investor has a fixed-consumption floor (i.e., a threshold standard of living).

---

[31]For decision-making criteria incorporating expected utility and Roy's safety-first rule, see Levy and Levy (2009). The authors provide a helpful review of the literature on decision-making criteria geared to maximize the probability of achieving a minimum acceptable economic result where any outcome falling short of this level constitutes an investment disaster.

[32]Risk aversion implies a diminishing marginal utility of wealth: The pleasure of gaining a dollar is less than the pain of losing a dollar. In this case, the pain of losing the opportunity to secure a dollar of periodic lifetime consumption is greater than the pleasure of realizing an extra dollar in each period.

Kingston and Thorp (2005) point out that the commonly used CRRA utility function is consistent only with a constant-mix portfolio management approach. HARA utility functions, however, can accommodate a buy-and-hold approach as well as convex payoff approaches, such as portfolio insurance and other dynamic asset allocation strategies. Any model using a CRRA utility function assumes that investors derive utility from consumption irrespective of its absolute level. However, it is plausible to assume that only consumption above a threshold level generates positive utility. When such a nonzero consumption floor is introduced into the model, a HARA utility function is, according to the authors, required to solve for the optimal strategy.[33] The presence of a consumption floor changes the decision-making process in that the goal can now be expressed in terms of surplus optimization.

In the Kingston–Thorp (2005) model, the minimum standard of living target is fully funded (escrowed) by the annuity. The primary motivation for adopting this strategy lies in the fact that the annuity contract's mortality premium makes it cheaper to escrow wealth earmarked to produce future income. The investor secures the floor income as soon as possible and, therefore, tends to favor early exercise of the option to annuitize.

This approach to portfolio design is a variation on Tobin's two-fund separation theorem, under which any feasible portfolio represents an investor's decision to allocate assets to an optimal risky asset fund and a risk-free asset. In the Kingston–Thorp solution, surplus wealth is invested in the risky-asset portfolio; the remainder is allocated to a risk-free annuity: "It follows that introducing a positive consumption floor has a similar effect to raising relative risk aversion. In addition, the agent recognizes that it is 'cheaper' to store escrow wealth in an annuity rather than a bond portfolio (at least where there are small enough loadings), creating another incentive to switch into complete annuitization at an earlier date" (Kingston and Thorp 2005, p. 234). Portfolio monitoring is critical in that a key ratio is the level of surplus relative to the changing costs of securing an acceptance-level income stream. The

---

[33]Technically, CRRA is nested in hyperbolic risk aversion functions. However, HARA functions encompass absolute risk aversion functions, such as decreasing absolute risk aversion (DARA), in which as wealth increases, the investor is more comfortable committing dollars to the risky asset; increasing absolute risk aversion (IARA), in which as wealth increases, the investor pulls back on the number of dollars put at risk; and constant absolute risk aversion (CARA), in which as wealth increases, the investor keeps the same amount of dollars at risk. Whenever the applicable risk metric defines the percentage of wealth put at risk, the risk model incorporates a *relative* risk aversion measure; whenever the applicable risk metric defines the level of dollar wealth put at risk, the risk model incorporates an *absolute* risk aversion measure. It is, however, the rare investor who remains indifferent to changes in the level of wealth when evaluating investment and spending strategies. This is a central criticism of incorporating a relative risk aversion measure into a utility-based model.

two-fund strategy—annuity plus risky-asset portfolio—also hearkens back to Korn and Krekel (2002). The reader may also recall Yaari's (1965) observation that annuity contracts permit investors to pursue separate solutions to the retirement income and the savings (bequest) problems.

A boundary control approach based on threshold levels of income or wealth shifts the portfolio control variable from asset allocation (long-term expected return) to the liability or spending variable. The feasibility condition for successful asset management depends on matching the investor's retirement assets to liabilities, where liabilities are expressed as the present value of future income, gifting, and bequest objectives. Dybvig's (1999) argument that efficient asset management requires a simultaneous solution of asset allocation and portfolio distribution policies reenters the academic discussion by the end of 2005.

We also take note of a plethora of articles seeking to back test the empirical distribution of realized investment returns to discover bright-line rules intended to enhance the safety and sustainability of retirement income portfolios. The studies, in general, apply one or more distribution formulas to various asset allocations in an attempt to uncover the optimal combination of spending and portfolio allocation. Early studies generally apply autopilot, fixed spending rules to static portfolio asset allocations. Later articles uncover flexible spending rules or dynamic asset allocation strategies that, if applied to the realized return sequence, would have enhanced retirement consumption and bequest goals during the historical period under evaluation. These articles are summarized and discussed in detail in Collins (2015).[34]

Additional Developments

Commentaries and debates on many of the issues we have mentioned also appear in journals written for readers in the estate and trust community. Although investment professionals may not often encounter these articles, the research has paramount importance for asset management within a fiduciary context.

In addition to the investment prudence standards embodied in federal ERISA (Employee Retirement Income Security Act of 1974) statutes, many states have adopted versions of the Uniform Prudent Investor Act, the Uniform Principal and Income Act, the Uniform Trust Code, and the Uniform Prudent Management of Institutional Funds Act. These uniform acts, as adopted by and embodied in specific state statutes, set standards of prudence for those investing trust-owned assets in a fiduciary capacity. Trustees of irrevocable family trusts are often charged with the duty to balance the interests of current (income) beneficiaries and those of remaindermen

---

[34]See http://schultzcollins.com/static/uploads/2015/07/Annotated-bibliography.pdf.

beneficiaries. Thus, the discussion regarding how to produce safe, substantial, and sustainable periodic income from a finite amount of capital while simultaneously preserving the value of terminal wealth has great import. Breaches of fiduciary duties may lead to substantial awards payable from a trustee's personal funds. A rich body of literature reflecting a broad heterogeneity of legal opinions provides valuable additional perspective.

By the mid-2000s, the academic discussions regarding portfolio management decisions split along several lines. One group of commentators advocates a bottom-up approach in which the investor annuitizes whenever he possesses sufficient wealth to lock in an acceptable threshold standard of living. Only surplus wealth is exposed to the risks and rewards of investing in the financial markets.

In contrast, a second group advocates a top-down approach in which the investor delays annuitization either until an optimal stopping time—the definition of "optimal" takes on various meanings depending on the financial risk metrics under investigation—or until it appears that the investor is dangerously close to the free boundary. The top-down advocates espouse an annuity-as-safety-net approach. There exists, of course, a spectrum of compromises—positions that recommend gradual annuitization based on various combinations of age, wealth, income, and bequest motivation triggers.

Irrespective of the suggestions flowing from a retirement income risk model, it is generally true that the greater the investment wealth relative to the demands placed on it, the more extensive the asset management choices. As wealth increases, Ezra (2009) notes, a surplus provides the luxury of focusing primarily on wealth management. If a decrease in wealth makes it necessary to hedge longevity risk, the annuitization option can then be considered. Academic modeling is rarely a perfect substitute for prudent judgment.

Part Two: Academic Research (2005–2014)

Modeling Additional Risk Factors and Input Variables

Many of the early academic papers construct risk models that, although they are mathematically elegant, incorporate major simplifying assumptions—complete markets, a representative investor exhibiting constant relative risk aversion, a lognormal return distribution. Recent studies tend to relax many of these assumptions, and the number of variables incorporated into risk models is larger. Horneff, Maurer, Mitchell, and Dus (2008) provide a comprehensive list of the important assumptions and variables that characterize risk models in the academic literature through 2007.

A good example of the way retirement portfolio models expand to encompass additional exogenous and endogenous variables is Horneff, Maurer and Stamos (2006). The authors consider (1) the impact of economic shocks on the demand to hold nonliquid annuity contracts, (2) human capital as a non-tradable asset that is a close substitute for bonds, and (3) other economic factors. Furthermore, their model is a continuous-time, barrier control–type problem that evaluates the option to annuitize throughout the entire life cycle as opposed to either a one-time option to annuitize at retirement or a continuously exercisable option only during retirement.

The consequence of incorporating a broader set of investor decisions into risk models is apparent in Milevsky and Young (2007). The authors point out that when an investor faces an all-or-nothing option to annuitize, the optimal time for annuitization of total wealth is when the expected return from the risky-asset portfolio equals the risk-free rate plus the annuity mortality credits. Under a CRRA assumption, "the optimal time to annuitize one's wealth is independent of wealth and is, therefore, deterministic" (p. 3148).

The decision rule thus states that when the value of the option to annuitize equals the expected value of the payoff from the underlying portfolio, then the option should be exercised. This is an option valuation problem. Beyond this time, any delay runs the risk of producing less future consumption than if the investor exercises the annuitization option immediately. The decision rule changes, however, in a model that gives an investor the capability of annuitizing a fraction of wealth at various time intervals: "The individual's optimal annuity purchasing is given by a barrier policy in that she will annuitize just enough of her wealth to stay on one side of the barrier in wealth-annuity space" (p. 3139). If wealth is spent to purchase an annuity, periodic income increases. In this risk model, the barrier's location is where the marginal utility of annuity income equals the marginal cost of spending down wealth to secure it. When the benefit of the income exceeds the benefit of retaining wealth, the investor will exercise the option to annuitize a fraction of wealth to restore equilibrium.

Both the implied and explicit financial planning recommendations appearing in the literature are model dependent, and with the rapid expansion of modeling capabilities, there is a marked increase in the heterogeneity of such recommendations. This shift puts a burden on the consumer of academic literature. The models, although quantitative in nature, do not generate conclusions that have the force and effect of mathematical theorems. Rather, increased complexity puts a premium on the reader's ability to understand a risk model's structure, assumptions, and input variables so that she can intelligently evaluate recommendations. Recommendations that are not empirical in nature are often replete with model risk, and a cautious investor rarely accepts them at face value.

Turra and Mitchell (2008) evaluate the utility of annuitization in the face of liquidity shocks. Even if the annuitant is in good health, "our stylized lifecycle model with uncertain out-of-pocket medical expenses shows that annuities become less attractive to people facing such medical expenses" (p. 246). This observation raises the issue of the attractiveness of annuities in an incomplete market setting: "When both adverse selection and uncertain medical expenses are accounted for and annuity markets are incomplete, we show that annuity equivalent wealth values are fairly low for people in poor health and about 25% higher for people in good health" (p. 246).[35]

The economic consequences of liquidity demands generated by a deterioration in health are also the focus of Ameriks, Caplin, Laufer, and Van Nieuwerburgh (2008). The authors conclude that the demand to annuitize *decreases* as wealth diminishes, in contrast to the annuity-as-safety-net school of thought. That is, they argue that there is a positive correlation between wealth and annuity demand. As financial resources shrink, the ability to fund lifestyle expenses diminishes. If an annuity purchase exhausts most liquid financial wealth, the investor incurs increased vulnerability to health shocks. At low-wealth levels, a serious medical shock would simultaneously deplete remaining assets, raise current expenses, and decrease the mortality-adjusted future value of existing annuity payments. If, as the authors suggest, "retirement security. . . can be summed up simply as 'having the resources you need, when you need them,'" then standard annuities may be only a partial solution to security in the face of severe health shocks: "Such products do little to deal with retirees' need for resources when emergencies arise, and they can even exacerbate financial distress in exigent situations" (pp. 271, 272).

---

[35]Part Three provides a more in-depth discussion of "annuity equivalent wealth."

A risk model that suggests a decrease in the demand to annuitize as wealth decreases also finds support Milevsky and Young (2007). They assert that the demand for annuities increases with wealth, risk aversion, positive health assessment, and portfolio volatility. Pang and Warshawsky (2010) argue that "the uncertainty in healthcare spending enhances the welfare gain of life annuities, more so for higher income households because such annuities are more likely to hedge their longer life and higher health spending" (p. 207).

We noted earlier that a large number of articles focus on the question of how much can be safely withdrawn each year from a retirement income portfolio. Some studies investigating "safe" withdrawal rates may mislead investors because they fail to account for a number of critical balance-sheet elements. On the plus side of the ledger, investors may own life insurance for the benefit of a surviving spouse or may expect an inheritance. Collins and Lam (2011) provide further insight on this topic.[36] On the minus side of the ledger are unreimbursed health costs and long-term care expenses. For example, Bajtelsmit, Foster, and Rappaport (2013) estimate that health and long-term care expenses add an extra $260,000 to overall costs of retirement for the average retired married couple. Retirement is expensive.

Bajtelsmit et al. (2013) consider households (husband age 66, wife age 63) at annual income levels of $60,000, $105,000, and $150,000. They evaluate three strategies for improving retirement income sustainability:

1. Delaying retirement

2. Cutting targeted spending

3. Acquiring long-term care insurance

The most effective tool is, by far, delaying the start of retirement. For all households, cutting spending by 15% has only a slight impact on the risk of running out of funds. The spending reduction benefit is easily overwhelmed either by poor investment performance or by high health costs. Their retirement income model suggests that long-term care (LTC) insurance produces limited benefits for the lowest-income households. It is generally an ineffective tool to enhance a higher-income household's financial security in retirement. The authors conclude that "based solely on the probability of having wealth remaining at death and the years without wealth, it appears that LTC insurance does more harm than good" (p. 322). Generally, "the LTC insurance premiums increased post-retirement expenses, resulting in quicker depletion of retirement wealth" (p. 322). The authors assert that "higher income families

---

[36]If insurance proceeds are available to the younger spouse, incorporating this contingent asset into the retirement income risk model may decrease shortfall probability significantly.

have enough wealth such that LTC costs do not play a substantial role in determining adequacy" (p. 327). For such high-income households, LTC contracts are not essential components of financial security.

In contrast, Blanchett (2014) indicates that retirement costs may be significantly less than many retirement income models suggest. He looks at data from several consumer spending surveys that track expenditures for households with retired investors.[37] The data reveal how household expenditures change, over time, at various ages. The rate of cost-of-living increases for seniors differs only modestly from that in the general population cost-of-living index: "From December 1982 to December 2012, the average annual change in the CPI-E (Consumer Price Index for the Elderly) has been 3.07% versus 2.92% for CPI-U (Consumer Price Index for Urban Consumers)" (p. 11).

Generally, according to surveys, retired investors spend neither a constant periodic dollar amount nor a constant amount adjusted for inflation. Rather, the cost curve is convex (shaped like a smile), with expenditures gradually decreasing with age until they move upward again toward the end of life. For example, the author cites one consumer spending study that finds that "consumption-expenditures decrease by about 2.5% when individuals retire; expenditures continue to decline at about a rate of 1% per year after that" (p. 6). Estimating expenditure curves for households at various income levels increases the accuracy of retirement cost projections. Compared with the outputs from traditional retirement income risk models, the true cost of retirement may be less. Blanchett asserts that "modeling the cost over the expected lifetime of the household, along with incorporating the actual spending curve, results in a required account balance at retirement that can be 25% less than the amount required using traditional models" (p. 23).

More and more investors are using online programs to calculate how much they can safely spend during retirement. Likewise, investment advisers frequently use retirement income–modeling software packages. If spending puts too much pressure on a retirement nest egg, the portfolio faces the risk of depletion during the investor's lifetime. However, as stated, when using retirement income–modeling applications, the investor must also consider model risk. Model risk is difficult to detect and, once spotted, is difficult to quantify. Turner and Witte (2009) conclude: "Notably, most programs do not do a good job of evaluating the risks that users face. . . . Generally most risks are ignored" (p. 12).[38]

A comprehensive look at the literature reveals a plethora of different research methods, modeling assumptions, and portfolio allocation and spending rules—all

---

[37]For a review of the empirical literature on spending during retirement, see Hurst (2008).
[38]This study is a follow-up to Society of Actuaries (2008), which provides risk management tables, suggestions, and comments for various types of risks faced by retirees.

of which may produce significantly different outputs even given the same empirical data. Conclusions are subject to model risk, and from time to time, practitioners may translate the output from academic model building—an exercise designed to explore quantitative relationships among variables of interest—into prescriptive statements for investors. But the mathematical assumptions required for tractable model building often diverge in both their character and form from common investor utility functions, from the process underlying the distribution of empirical asset price evolutions, or from any realistic pattern of retiree spending decisions. Conversely, from time to time, practitioner-oriented articles may resort to pure empiricism in an attempt to parse historical return evolutions to find rules for safe and sustainable portfolio withdrawals.

Although historical back testing continues to appear in some recent articles, there is a growing awareness of its limitations. Researchers are now more likely to use either

- shortfall probability analysis—generally derived from a Monte Carlo simulation model—or

- utility-based analysis that optimizes one or more objective functions within a life-cycle model.

Unfortunately, the substantive differences in model outputs can confuse investors and financial advisers alike. For example, under one retirement income–modeling approach, an annuity may appear as an expensive and undesirable retirement planning instrument; another approach may characterize annuitization as a worthwhile asset management option. A heightened awareness of model risk is useful in that it diminishes the propensity to base financial strategy on any one risk measure or model type.

An awareness of risk model limitations informs an interesting essay by Blanchett (2013). Although the underlying risk model is simplistic, Blanchett's work is noteworthy because it incorporates multiple approaches to quantifying the risks and rewards of retirement income strategies. Blanchett begins by reminding readers that the buyer of an annuity should expect to bear a cost in excess of its actuarially fair value. Today's low interest rates increase the cost of periodic income because the insurance carriers cannot earn substantial amounts on their underlying bond investments. However, even in the absence of a positive expected present value, an annuity buyer may experience an increase in welfare.

Blanchett (2013) presents a table of sustainable withdrawal rates derived from a Monte Carlo simulation model assuming fixed 3% inflation, constant-dollar withdrawal rates based on percentages ranging from 3% to 10% of initial value, and a $1 million initial portfolio value. Planning horizons range from 20 to 40 years. For example, according to the model, at a 4% real withdrawal rate, there is a 9% chance of portfolio depletion by the end of a fixed 30-year period. Adding the condition of survivorship of at least one spouse over the 30-year planning horizon drops the failure rate to 8%, assuming a 65-year-old couple. Not all 65-year-old couples will survive over the full period.

The challenge faced by the retiring household is to determine whether the potential benefits of an annuity outweigh the costs. Blanchett (2013) calculates annuity internal rates of return (IRRs) for a male, a female, and a couple (100% survivorship benefit), assuming they are 65 years old at the time of annuitization. The calculations indicate that IRRs for all groups become positive by approximately age 80. An early death results in a highly negative IRR; a long life may result in a modestly positive IRR. The IRR distribution has a pronounced left-side skew: "From a practical perspective, the negative skew associated with IRRs. . . should be viewed as the 'cost' of offsetting the potential positive skew associated with life expectancy. The annuitant is effectively trading the possibility of dying early (and the corresponding negative IRRs) with the hedge of living a long life and having guaranteed income the entire period" (p. 47).

Blanchett (2013) supplements the IRR analysis with a utility-based analysis. The model's utility function reflects CRRA and is the standard von Neumann–Morgenstern power utility function, over which an investor maximizes expected utility calculated over a probability distribution of potential outcomes.[39] Blanchett's model characterizes utility as a function of the income goal replacement ratio achieved during retirement. This ratio is the present value of all payments received over the retiree's lifetime, plus the balance remaining at death, divided by the present value of the total income goal or need. This calculation, of course, considers aggregate utility across the planning horizon rather than period-by-period utility achieved by income in excess of the threshold target. However, Blanchett incorporates a term to reflect the investor's aversion to income variance: "The utility-maximizing portfolio will be the combination of assets that both maximizes retirement income and minimizes the downside variability associated with generating the income" (p. 48).

The portfolio under consideration has a mean return of 7% with a standard deviation of 9%. This is characteristic, according to Blanchett (2013), of a portfolio with a 40% allocation to stocks and 60% to bonds. Returns are lognormally distributed. Each retiree (male, female, or couple) has an inflation-adjusted withdrawal of $30,000 per year (and is assumed to survive throughout

---

[39]An investor seeking to maximize expected utility is said to be von Neumann–Morgenstern rational, provided that the utility function satisfies certain axioms of rational choice, including transitivity, independence, continuity, and completeness. If a rational investor's utility function satisfies these conditions, the investor will select the investment strategy offering the statistically greatest likelihood of providing the highest amount of utility (welfare).

the study period). If the annuity provides more than the targeted withdrawal rate, the excess is reinvested into the stock/bond portfolio. Results are tested at the currently available annuity rates and for alternative annuity pricing factors that assume interest rates of 50 bps and 100 bps higher. The utility-based analysis concludes: "An IFA [immediate fixed annuity] is not [optimal under] any of the current rate scenarios [for those annuitizing] under age 70, and [appears] only with material allocations for those annuitizing at age 80. However, the optimal allocation to an IFA does increase at older ages, and increases considerably should IFA rates improve" (p. 49). For example, at a 4% initial portfolio withdrawal rate, a male should forgo annuitization until approximately age 75. At that time, 30% of the portfolio should be annuitized. Blanchett writes: "Given today's annuitization rates, which are currently near all-time lows, many retirees are likely better off waiting until interest rates and subsequent annuitization rates improve, or delaying the IFA purchase decision to an older age. Even with today's low rates, IFAs remain an attractive longevity hedge for retirees age 80 or older" (p. 49).

Blanchett's model is rudimentary, but it is instructive to note the sensitivity of normative statements not only to changes in model input values and variables but also to modeling approaches (cost-of-retirement efficiency criteria versus utility of consumption).

Although we do not cover the topic of compensation for incurring liquidity risk when contracting for an annuity, we acknowledge that the cost of illiquidity will vary from investor to investor and may be substantial. We refer the interested reader to Amihud and Mendelson (1986) who attempt to quantify the costs of illiquidity, and to the many successive studies published in the late 1980s and thereafter.

The subjects of model risk, modeling approaches, and portfolio shortfall probability analysis under various spending regimes receive comprehensive treatment in Collins, Lam, and Stampfli (2015a). The authors take note of the proclivity of many researchers to present conclusions from models that pile up a series of indefensible assumptions, such as a constant rate of inflation, time-invariant volatility, fixed correlation matrices, Gaussian distribution of future investment returns, and so forth. On the plus side, many such papers pose interesting and important questions; on the minus, many present spurious conclusions. Readers interested in exploring this literature are also referred to Collins (2015).

Life-Cycle Models, Control Variables, and Portfolio Sustainability

The utility of consumption and bequest models—especially the classic life-cycle models—offer valuable insight into complex interactions among longevity, asset allocation, labor income, work/leisure trade-offs, timing of annuitization options, and portfolio withdrawal strategies (investor spending). Optimal asset allocation and portfolio management decisions vary substantially across the population of investors depending on (1) the form of the investor's utility of wealth function (e.g., relative or absolute risk aversion) and (2) the degree of investor risk aversion (i.e., the concavity of the utility function). In general, the life-cycle model research shreds conventional wisdom regarding one-size-fits-all rules of portfolio design and management. There appears to be neither an optimal allocation for all seasons nor an optimal withdrawal rule for all portfolios.

Asset Management Control Variables: Retirement Spending. The amount and timing of retirement spending is, not surprisingly, an important factor in estimating the likelihood that a portfolio will be able to provide adequate lifetime income. Spending—or, more precisely, spending flexibility—is a key control variable in many retirement income risk models. For example, Milevsky and Robinson (2005) assert that retirement is feasible when current wealth is greater than the stochastic present value (SPV) of a spending plan. A retirement plan's success or failure is affected by age, asset allocation, and spending target. The authors test which of these three levers of retirement sustainability is of greatest importance in preventing retirement ruin. In general, they find spending rates higher than 5% of initial wealth produce unacceptably high probabilities of ruin. The spending decision dominates the asset allocation decisions at a 5+% rate: "No matter what reasonable portfolio is chosen, asset allocation will not turn a bad situation into a good one" because return and variance move together and any attempt to increase return also increases the failure rate (p. 97). The two most effective levers for controlling retirement success, according to Milevsky and Robinson, are (1) postponement of portfolio distributions to a later age and (2) reductions in consumption targets. The authors' findings represent a change in emphasis from Milevsky's (1998) earlier option valuation approach; asset management now focuses on monitoring wealth relative to the SPV of consumption.

Smith and Gould (2007) test the effect of a flexible withdrawal policy on shortfall probability. Their model assumes a 50% elasticity of spending; a 10% change in wealth generates a 5% change (in the same direction) in spending. The flexible spending policy dominates the fixed withdrawal rule because it produces less shortfall risk and higher terminal wealth across all allocations. Flexibility in spending (elasticity of consumption) is a critical factor in portfolio sustainability in this model.

Follow-on studies incorporating flexible spending into a retirement income risk model include Stout (2008), Spitzer (2008), and Milevsky and Huang (2011).

Mitchell (2011) tests a set of withdrawal rules customized to the investor's risk–reward preferences and cash flow objectives. The application of the rules is a function of dynamically changing portfolio values as well as expected remaining lifetime of the investor. Mitchell notes that "anticipating adverse events and taking corrective action increases our chances of avoiding larger more catastrophic problems" (p. 45). In this case, the event to be avoided is financial ruin. Mitchell bases his withdrawal rules on the ratio between the present value of an annuity calculated for the remaining *expected* life of the retired investor and the portfolio's *initial* value.[40] Additionally, Mitchell's discount rate for calculating the PV of the annuity is the historical rate earned by the risky-asset portfolio—not the rate associated with a historical, current, or estimated yield curve. Under Mitchell's approach, a shortfall probability metric trumps a utility of consumption metric.

An upper threshold (UT) term in the equation determines how much "excess" value must exist before a change in withdrawal rate should be considered by the investor. Unless the ratio of a portfolio's current mortality-adjusted annuity value multiplied by the portfolio's original value exceeds the portfolio's current value by the UT amount, no change occurs in the withdrawal rate. Mitchell (2011) also introduces a downside threshold (DT). A DT of 1.5, for example, requires the portfolio to have a 50% excess over the discounted, mortality-adjusted value of the expected lifetime withdrawal income stream. The factor for the portfolio's original value is not present in the DT calculation. A higher DT is more conservative, in the sense that there must be a greater amount of excess value before withdrawals can be increased.

Mitchell advocates a conservative initial consumption policy. If future portfolio returns are positive, a higher portfolio value may allow for increasing dollar withdrawals—a start-low/go-high withdrawal strategy. Complex rules, in Mitchell's opinion, are required because of asset price volatility. There is a maximum (MAX) and minimum (MIN) allowable withdrawal rate under all economic environments. Ongoing asset management controls focus on the percentage of increase or decrease that can be actually withdrawn in any one period: "For example, if a retiree amortizes their portfolio over their expected remaining lifespan at historic rates of return and finds the portfolio could sustain a 10% withdrawal rate as compared to a current 6% withdrawal rate, a 40% UR (upward adjustment rate) would allow them to only increase the withdrawal rate to 7.6% that is $\left\{6\% + \left[0.4 \times (10\% - 6\%)\right]\right\}$ " (p. 49).

Mitchell (2011) uses Stout and Mitchell (2006) as a base case for comparison purposes. He calculates that application of the controls yields a 6.63%

---

[40]The ratio mixes a forward-looking numerator with a backward-looking denominator.

average withdrawal rate, 4.33% probability of ruin to age 100, and averaging ending real portfolio value 1.07 times the beginning amount based on 1926–2004 data. The same controls, updated to 2008, yield a 6.47% average withdrawal rate, 8.68% probability of ruin to age 100 and average ending real portfolio value 0.88 times the beginning amount. "Thus, merely incorporating two years' more results (including a major market crash) into the underlying dataset means that there is an approximate doubling of the portfolio failure rate. . ..What is optimal today may not be tomorrow; presumably because of heteroskedasticity" (Mitchell 2011, p. 49). Mitchell, however, acknowledges that his rules-based system does not comfortably coexist with a utility of consumption preference-based system: "Retirees may prefer greater consumption at younger ages when they are more active. . . at the expense of reduced consumption if they superannuate" (p. 53).

The start-low/go-high withdrawal strategy recommendation is a consequence of heightened attention to sequence risk (i.e., a series of returns below expected return) and to the consequences of sequence risk on the risk-of-ruin probability. As noted, however, conservative initial portfolio withdrawal rates are vulnerable to criticism from (1) authors of research studies who incorporate a utility penalty for deviations on both the low and high side of targeted benchmark income and (2) authors who use utility-based life-cycle models that, when incorporating a factor for high-subjective discounting (investor impatience), assert that optimal retirement spending often decreases with age.

Although a review of the literature reveals that many commentators advocate a start-low/go-high withdrawal strategy, this approach comes under full-scale assault in Pye (2012). The mundane topic of how to monitor and manage a retirement income portfolio to fund future current and future spending is becoming controversial. We devote a separate section to Pye's work.

We also call attention to Frank, Mitchell, and Blanchett (2011) as an additional example of a retirement portfolio risk model that tracks a shortfall risk metric but also concurrently evaluates the marginal utility of income as a function of attained age. The authors' retirement income model focuses on portfolio withdrawals as the critical control variable. At the start of retirement, the investor sets a probability-of-failure rate that matches her risk tolerance preferences. Future withdrawal rates (WR%) are managed so that the probability of failure (POF) rate remains constant over time: "The WR%s are managed so that the retiree has a target exposure to the POF rates (e.g., 5% probability of failure at age "x" at a y% withdrawal rate). . . . A set withdrawal rate (e.g., 4%) is not optimal for all retirees because not all retirees are the same *age*)" (p. 9). In the authors' opinion, "de-cumulation should be viewed as a dynamic, rather than set-and-forget, exercise" (p. 11).

A Shift in Emphasis Leads to a New Benchmark—and to Conflicting Recommendations. The authors cited in the previous section emphasize the importance of prudent spending policy in mitigating the risk of portfolio depletion prior to the end of the planning horizon. The focus on spending—especially the introduction of a threshold periodic income target—rather than on terminal wealth has a number of important consequences. A threshold income requires a change in the utility function. We will pick up the threads of this discussion shortly within the context of dynamically changing risk aversion. Most importantly, however, the control variable is now the retired investor's standard of living itself. Utility and shortfall risk metrics converge to a "hurdle race" problem where the solution requires both long-term portfolio sustainability *and* success in providing a minimum period-by-period income. The actuarial literature outlined in Part One of this literature review commands increased attention as investigation into the techniques for and costs of producing adequate income throughout the planning horizon becomes most important.

At least two issues emerge: (1) a benchmarking issue—to what extent the annuity benchmark represents a reasonable way to compare and contrast retirement income strategies—and (2) a debate regarding the prudence of when and how to incorporate annuitization into the management of retirement assets. Neither issue is new. However, the incorporation of a threshold income requirement into risk modeling changes the nature of the investigation. For example, Huang and Milevsky (2008) assert that the minimum amount of income needed by the family unit over the life cycle is the main driver of the demand for either life insurance coverage or income annuities. Sustaining a target level of periodic income is the appropriate measure of financial risk.

Commentators continue to split on whether to (1) annuitize as soon as possible lest a forthcoming bear market jeopardize the ability to secure threshold income or (2) delay annuitization to capture the expected equity risk premium and, potentially, enter into a lower-cost annuity contract issued at an older age. We term the first asset management strategy the "annuitize ASAP strategy" and the second, the "annuity-as-safety-net strategy." In starker terms, the choice is between (1) annuitizing now and resolving ambiguities surrounding the sources and amount of future income or (2) waiting to annuitize as long as a delay remains a prudent and suitable investment management election.

A good example of the ASAP strategy is Babbel and Merrill (2007). The authors suggest that a utility-maximizing investor will not pursue a strategy that leaves a positive probability of failing to support a threshold level of lifetime consumption. Penetrating this minimum produces, in their opinion, infinite disutility, and given the assumption that utility is additive across all economic states, such a strategy is irrational.[41] Their model directs the investor to allocate risk-free assets sufficient to support the minimum periodic income goal. In a multiperiod context, the risk-free asset is an inflation-adjusted annuity like Social Security.

If the minimum consumption target requires periodic income greater than that available through government or corporate pension benefits, the Babbel and Merrill (2007) model advises the investor to annuitize immediately a portion of current wealth to fund the deficit. Excess wealth remains invested in a financial asset portfolio. Investors annuitize up to the point where the marginal utility of an extra dollar of consumption equals the marginal disutility of spending down wealth to fund an annuity income. For investors with average risk aversion parameters, annuity loads have, in the authors' opinion, minimal impact on the allocation decision, provided that the markups above the actuarially fair price are less than 30%.

The Babbel and Merrill (2007) model is interesting for a number of additional reasons. First, it incorporates a HARA utility function by virtue of a minimum required income floor, and it assumes that the investor allocates risk-free assets sufficient to support the minimum standard of living goal. Second, in a multiperiod context, the risk-free asset is an inflation-adjusted annuity. The authors argue for a bottom-up asset management approach, in which the investor, with little or no delay, converts financial assets into an annuity designed to provide threshold income. Only surplus wealth is allocated to a risky-asset portfolio—a buy-an-annuity-and-invest-the-difference strategy. If the amount of wealth allocated to the annuity is large, however, the investor may not have remaining funds sufficient to implement the optimal allocation to the risky-asset portfolio. Assuming that the risky-asset portfolio has a higher expected return than the annuity portfolio, the decrease in aggregate expected return (disutility) must be balanced against reduced uncertainty in future consumption (utility). The authors point out that the feedback loop plus the wealth constraint make an analytic solution impossible.[42]

---

[41]The next section explores the topic of utility in greater detail. For now, we simply note that it is important to distinguish among models assuming static risk aversion throughout the planning horizon; dynamically changing risk aversion throughout the planning horizon; a state-preference utility function within each interval throughout the horizon; and, finally, a nonseparable, nonadditive utility of wealth function, perhaps based on a preference for maintaining the investor's historical standard of living. The key point is that different assumptions regarding the appropriate and applicable utility function lead to profoundly different preferencing criteria and hence to significant differences in the ranking of investment/withdrawal strategies derived from retirement income risk models.

[42]Analytic solutions are efficient and relatively easy. However, they cannot be used with multiple sources of complexity or with sequences of investment/spending decisions.

In contrast to Babbel and Merrill (2007), Fullmer (2007) espouses a top-down approach, where the option to annuitize is a last-resort safety measure. Fullmer asserts that systematic withdrawal plans must often reduce future spending following a bear market. However, "this amounts to managing longevity risk through spending management. This approach sacrifices the investor's standard of living in the event of poor market returns" (p. 1).

The case for retirement income portfolios is unlike the modern portfolio theory approach to asset accumulation, where the investor is concerned with terminal wealth and where standard deviation of wealth is an appropriate risk metric. Rather, according to Fullmer (2007), a more appropriate risk measure is the sustainability of income sufficient to support a threshold standard of living. Shortfall risk, relative to this threshold standard, is a more meaningful risk metric to the investor. However, a probability measure of the likelihood of achieving a sustainable threshold is not an ideal risk measure because it fails to take into account the magnitude of failure should the threshold be breached. The author asserts that the best strategy for managing retirement income risk is to annuitize when necessary—but not before, which puts him squarely in the annuity-as-safety-net camp.

The key to implementing a prudent portfolio management strategy is to evaluate continuously the option to annuitize financial assets. By exercising the option only when it is necessary to ensure a threshold standard of living, the investor takes full advantage of the time value of the annuitization option. Fullmer (2007) writes: "The key for leveraging this optionality is setting the projected cost to annuitize the investor's desired lifetime income stream as a *wealth* goal in the objective function. Doing so effectively transforms longevity risk into investment risk, because now it is the portfolio's job to preserve the ability to annuitize the desired lifetime income stream. . . . By monitoring the investor's wealth relative to the current cost of annuitization, the decision to invest or annuitize can be continually evaluated by a financial adviser" (p. 6).

This logic leads directly to a recommendation for "a dynamic allocation strategy" (p. 9). Fullmer (2007) asserts, "When substantial cash flow risk is present, the objective function begins to take on more of the characteristics of a cash flow matching model" (p. 9). The risk management approach mirrors the hurdle race problem in which the "provision" must exceed the cost of securing the threshold living standard through annuitization. The author terms this an "annuitization hurdle" (p. 10). This threshold wealth standard is a more appropriate benchmark against which to measure the risk of shortfall than complete portfolio depletion, which measures the risk of ruin: "Portfolio values below zero represent financial ruin, while values below the annuitization hurdle represent an inability to fund the desired annuity" (p. 10).

Under this risk management approach, the investor monitors the cost of buying an annuity to fund threshold income and compares this cost with the market value of assets remaining in the portfolio. The decision becomes how much of the portfolio surplus to put at risk before exercising the option to annuitize. Fullmer (2007) also provides a refreshing counterpoint to the conventional wisdom that suggests a retiree with dwindling resources must assume more risk in the hope that the portfolio will bounce back from bear market declines.

We note, additionally, that Fullmer's (2007) opinion regarding the drawbacks of the shortfall risk measure predates arguments made by Kitces (2012). Kitces asserts that "the plan with the lowest risk of adjustment may not be the ideal plan for the client" (p. 1). A plan with a relatively low risk of adjustment may require a draconian adjustment conditional on the adjustment requirement. Alternately, a plan with a higher risk of adjustment may require a less disruptive change in retirement income: "In other words, it may be better to follow the plan that leads to a slow failure—which can be easily fixed with mid-course adjustments—than a fast failure" (p. 3). Kitces, like Fullmer, believes that the investor must consider both the risk of adjustment and the potential magnitude of the adjustment.

Finally, we call attention to a Gupta and Li (2007) study. The authors contribute to the annuity-as-safety-net approach to portfolio management. High levels of wealth diminish the demand for annuitization of financial assets. Additionally, their model locates an upper bound for the age of annuitization because of brevity risk, meaning that the length of the planning horizon becomes a factor in the decision to annuitize. A sudden change in health may cause an annuitization decision to have poor results (i.e., the annuitant may not live to collect many payments), which would decrease investor utility. It is interesting to note how Frank et al. (2011) further develop the Gupta and Li insights into an aged-based utility of consumption portfolio preferencing criterion.

Utility—Again. Each investor has a unique utility of wealth function. It is often convenient to use a power utility function, with the most commonly used exponent of 0.5—quadratic utility. Alternately, utility of wealth can be expressed using a logarithmic function.[43] Thus, an investor may express the value of $100 as the square root of 100 (that is, 10 utiles), assuming a quadratic curve in wealth/utility space, or as the natural log of 100 (4.61 utiles), assuming a logarithmic curve.

---

[43]Log utility's slope approaches zero at the limit of infinite wealth and approaches negative infinity at zero wealth. An exponent of 1 signifies a risk-neutral investor. Quadratic utility is similar, but not identical, to mean–variance utility.

Each exponent value generates a curve with differing slope values across the wealth spectrum. The first derivative of the slope at each point along the curve measures the marginal utility of a unit of money at that point. With the exception of gamblers' utility curves, a utility curve is concave with a positive first derivative (i.e., more wealth is better) and a negative second derivative (i.e., the pain of a dollar loss is greater than the pleasure of a dollar gain). The slope value, therefore, measures an investor's sensitivity to gains or losses at any given wealth level. When wealth is low, the marginal utility of an extra dollar is high, and vice versa. Risk aversion is the reciprocal of the marginal utility of wealth and is usually incorporated into risk models with a negative exponent value to reflect the fact that it occupies a position in the denominator of the fraction.

An economic interpretation of the first and second derivatives is as follows: The first derivative indicates how the investor's utility itself changes as wealth increases or decreases; the second derivative indicates the extent to which the investor's marginal utility, or rate at which the investor converts wealth to utility, is changing as wealth increases or decreases. Thus, risk aversion is the elasticity of marginal utility with respect to wealth.

Students of finance are familiar with risk aversion curves primarily through the ubiquitous illustrations of Harry Markowitz's technique for locating the optimal portfolio at the intersection of the efficient frontier and the highest investor indifference curve. Indifference curves are risk aversion curves. The steepness of the indifference curve determines its point of tangency with the set of efficient portfolios, and the steepness, in turn, is a function of each investor's risk aversion. In the case of mean–variance utility, the optimum is achieved by finding the highest feasible indifference curve. When either utility of wealth (i.e., the ability to make gifts and bequests) or utility of consumption (i.e., the ability to meet periodic income targets throughout the planning horizon) is an important preferencing criterion, it is of utmost importance to recognize that model outputs may be extremely sensitive to the nature and form of the implied utility/risk aversion function(s).[44]

It is useful to distinguish among

- models that assume static risk aversion throughout the planning horizon;

- those that assume dynamically changing risk aversion throughout the planning horizon;

- those that assume a state-preference utility function within each interval throughout the horizon; and

---

[44]Utility of bequests, gifting, and consumption may differ. A good review of utility functions, their derivatives, and their role in financial economics is found in Sharpe (2007).

- those that assume a nonseparable, nonadditive utility of wealth function perhaps based on a preference for maintaining the investor's historical standard of living.

The key point is that different assumptions regarding the appropriate and applicable utility function lead to profoundly different rankings of investment/ withdrawal strategies derived from retirement income risk model outputs.

Many utility-based retirement income models assume a CRRA function for several reasons:

- Such a function assumes that the investor is willing to invest a constant fraction of wealth in a risky-asset portfolio irrespective of the actual level of wealth at any moment in time (i.e., CRRA is wealth invariant). This greatly simplifies the mathematics required to achieve a solution to the risk model.

- CRRA approximates, under a range of conditions, mean–variance utility under which an investor cares only about the first two moments of the distribution of returns. This allows the model builder to assume a normal distribution of returns, which, in turn, also simplifies the mathematics.

- When only the first two moments of a return distribution's are portfolio choice factors, the Sharpe ratio becomes a permissible performance evaluation metric and the optimal weight in the risky asset is given by the Merton optimum.

- CRRA utility allows for the application of classic von Neumann–Morgenstern–Savage axioms of utility. For any risk aversion value, the model builder can compute the wealth certainty equivalent, which permits a cardinal ranking of asset management approaches from models generating aggregate consumption and terminal wealth utility values.

Unfortunately, although the CRRA function has many useful modeling properties, it also has a variety of well-known shortcomings. As noted, the introduction of a floor or threshold amount of wealth or income demands functions like the HARA function or a state-preference utility function. State-preference utility assumes that an individual wishes to avoid low-consumption levels during bad economic periods. A dollar in a recessionary economy is more highly valued than a dollar during a period of prosperity. Similarly, when a retiree is interested in smoothing consumption over time, the model builder might wish to distinguish risk aversion in a single period from intertemporal risk aversion by using an Epstein–Zin utility function. The Epstein–Zin function uses an additional term to represent the elasticity of intertemporal substitution (EIS). Highly risk-averse investors have a low value of EIS because they wish to avoid large swings in consumption from one period to the next. A critical risk metric to track in models using Epstein–Zin utility is multiperiod consumption variance.

Behavioral theories of finance posit that investors exhibit loss aversion, which can introduce convexity into the utility function as wealth drops beneath a critical value or reference point. In addition to the family of utility functions described by Venter (1983), a variety of other utility functions—including Fisher (1930) utility and habit or standard of living utility—are found in retirement income risk models.

A good example of a study that compares conclusions based on a model assuming CRRA utility to conclusions derived from other utility functions, including habit utility, is Davidoff et al. (2003). They begin by pointing out that the classic Yaari (1965) life-cycle consumer with no bequest objective and with an uncertain date of death annuitizes all wealth under the assumption that the consumer is an expected utility maximizer with intertemporally separable utility and with access to actuarially fair annuity products.[45] The authors, however, contend that it is not necessary to assume that the consumer is an exponential discounter or that he obeys the standard von Neumann–Morgenstern–Savage utility axioms or for the annuity to be actuarially fair. Consumers, under a Yaari-like model, will annuitize all wealth, provided that they have no bequest motives and that the net rate of return on the annuities is greater than the return on conventional assets of matching financial risk.[46]

Under models incorporating other utility functions, however, immediate annuitization may not be optimal. The authors present a simulation model for a single 65-year-old male. Their model assumes a power utility function, exponential discounting at a deterministic rate, and general population mortality. They calculate four welfare measures after applying the model to investors with both separable utility and standard of living utility:

1. Increase in wealth required to hold utility constant while moving from a constant real annuity to conventional bonds

2. Fraction of wealth optimally committed to real annuities instead of bonds

3. Increase in wealth required to hold utility constant while moving from optimal annuity position to conventional bonds

---

[45]Utility of consumption in period two does not depend on the investor's consumption (standard of living) in period one. Each period's utility can be estimated separately with aggregate utility, defined as the sum of all separately evaluated periods.

[46]That is, investors with intertemporally separable preferences, log utility, and a discount rate equal to the risk-free rate.

4. Gain in utility from selecting the optimal payout trajectory (bonds or annuities) with no requirement for either

The assumption regarding market completeness turns out to be especially important in the decision to purchase an actuarially fair annuity. Annuities are illiquid and may not generate sufficient funds in the event of a liquidity crisis that may arise from such emergencies as uninsured medical expenses. Consumers are willing to commit to a fixed plan of expenditures at a starting time only if they are able to trade goods across all periods and all states of nature (i.e., trading is a means of reversing or revising initial decisions). But an annuity, by definition, is an irreversible contract. Thus, the standard way to assess an annuity's benefit overstates its utility value. Generally, the authors' model suggests that the greater the wealth, the lower the demand to annuitize. The incompleteness of markets may render annuitization of a large fraction of wealth suboptimal. In terms of the ASAP versus safety net debate, the Davidoff et al. (2003) model provides support for delaying annuitization and indicates when it is prudent to do so.

Furthermore, according to Davidoff et al. (2003), some studies do not capture the utility loss from locking in a fixed periodic income. In one sense, annuities are costly because they contribute to consumption constraints: "The welfare effects of larger increases in annuitization are more difficult to sign (that is, to determine whether positive or negative) because they may constrain consumption" (p. 21). Full annuitization may distort consumption (i.e., place an upper bound on feasible future consumption) and, therefore, may not be optimal, especially when utility is measured relative to the level of past consumption (i.e., standard of living). The utility of living in a studio apartment is different for a person who has lived in one throughout her life than for someone who lived in a mansion during previous years. The authors contend that investors trade off consumption between periods based not only on budget constraints but also on standard of living ratios. Marginal utility of consumption in any period incorporates two effects not present in the additively separable utility model:

1. The effect of present standard of living on present marginal utility

2. The effect of present consumption on future period utility

The authors conclude that the interaction of various model components—the form of the utility function, the assumption of complete markets, and the extent of budget constraints—makes it difficult to estimate the welfare benefits of annuitization.

Huang and Milevsky (2008) also abandon strict reliance on a CRRA function in favor of modeling preferences using a HARA function. The HARA function is appropriate for a model generating utility values only at or above the floor consumption targets. Indeed, the authors concede that maximizing utility over all investment outcomes is less than ideal, and they note that using a state-dependent utility calculation would be more realistic. This observation mirrors, in some respects, the issues raised in Vanduffel et al. (2003).

Balls (2006) provides a model featuring a risk aversion parameter that changes as a function of changing health states. Balls's utility-based model assumes discounting of contingent future consumption (i.e., the model weights the utility of consumption by the probability that the investor is alive to enjoy it). The author develops an annuitant mortality model: "Optimal consumption decision is derived for the case where no annuity market exists. Using the same utility framework, we derive the threshold price for an immediate annuity" (p. 104). The model, however, focuses primarily on the health state of the potential annuitant as opposed to chronological age. The health state in any period can improve or deteriorate according to a transition probability modeled by a Markov transition matrix.[47] Transition probabilities are calibrated by maximizing a log likelihood function from the data in the US Census population mortality tables for the years 1900–1990.

Balls (2006) incorporates the health transition process into an economic model in which the utility of consumption in each period is influenced by the annuitant's health state. Bequests are not considered. Per-period utility, conditional on health state *j*, is defined as:

$$U_j\left(c_t\right) = K_c + \left(\alpha + 1\right)^{-1}\left(\theta_j c_t\right)^{\alpha+1},$$

where *c* is consumption, θ is a health-state consumption modifier, $\alpha \leq 0$ is the risk aversion parameter, and *K* is a utility constant whose sole purpose is to make utility positive. The author acknowledges that the choice of the utility function (constant relative risk aversion) "is based on mathematical simplicity. . . . Relative risk aversion (risk aversion divided by consumption or wealth) is constant" (p. 108). In a market where the consumer has access to annuities, "the value of wealth is simply the utility value of the annuity purchased with the assets" (p. 111).

Balls's (2006) model solves for the payout rate that the annuity must provide so that the utility of annuitized wealth exactly equals the expected utility

---

[47]A Markov transition process multiplies a matrix of values in an "initial state" by a probability vector that represents the likelihood of transitioning to different values in the next state. This transition process continues until or unless the matrix reaches an equilibrium state or a final state condition—that is, all members of a population are deceased. For further discussion of Markov matrices in an investment context, see Collins et al. (2015a).

of lifetime consumption given the investor's current health state, risk aversion coefficient, and time-preference discount rate. For example, an investor in the best health state, with a risk aversion coefficient of −1.50 and a 2% time discount preferencing rate, requires an annuity payout rate of 5.41% per year when the expected rate of return on invested assets is 5%. A person in the worst living health state is indifferent between maintaining the portfolio with an expected return of 5% and annuitizing wealth with a payout rate of 11.88%.

Changing the risk aversion coefficient to reflect greater risk aversion changes the indifference rates: "The higher the risk-aversion parameter, the greater the policyholder's premium for retirement risk protection" (p. 111). Changing the health-state consumption modifier to a state-dependent variable indicates that a constant annuity payout is no longer optimal. According to Balls (2006), an annuity is optimal if payments to the annuitant increase as lower health states emerge. The model confirms that there "are advantages to delaying annuitization, particularly when market returns available to the policyholder are superior to those available in the form of an annuity. However, the effect here is heterogeneous, depending also on the expected longevity of the policyholder" (p. 113).

These findings mirror those of Davidoff et al. (2003), who find that the incompleteness of markets may render annuitization of a large fraction of wealth suboptimal. Balls (2006) is also significant in that the author expands the definition of risk aversion to include a factor for what Gupta and Li (2007) call "brevity risk." We note two apparent points:

1. Realistic modeling of the dynamics of retirement income portfolios is becoming increasingly complex.

2. Prescriptive advice changes significantly with the choice of input variables, with the form of the assumed utility function, and with assumptions regarding stochastic modeling of investment return and inflation processes.[48]

New Definitions of Prudent Asset Management. Modeling retirement income portfolios under the stress of fees and distributions rapidly turns to considerations of asset/liability management. Incorporating a wealth-invariant CRRA function operating over the entire wealth domain becomes increasingly problematic. Many commentators begin to define prudent asset management in terms of synchronizing the projected costs of targeted spending relative to the portfolio's current wealth level. Prudence is no longer exclusively defined as an optimal time to exercise annuitization options, an asset management rule of thumb (e.g., tilting the allocation toward stocks improves

---

[48]Collins and Stampfli (2009) provide a more detailed discussion in the context of management of assets owned by irrevocable trusts.

long-term portfolio sustainability), or a bright-line spending rule (e.g., the 4% of initial portfolio value rule adjusted for subsequent changes in inflation).

A good example of the shift in approach to retirement income modeling is Gerrard, Haberman, and Vigna (2006), an update to Gerrard et al. (2004). The authors assume (1) that current wealth is insufficient to purchase an annuity at the desired level of consumption and (2) that the retiree elects to invest in risky assets with the hope of achieving a more favorable future income stream. There is a subtle, yet important, rephrasing of the investment issues. The problem is now expressed as risking ruin to achieve a future wealth goal, where the objective is to maximize the probability of attaining the goal while minimizing the probability of bankruptcy.

The question, of course, is whether this strategy is prudent. Gerrard et al. (2006) argue for constant monitoring of fund size relative to its ability to support performance targets. Their normative model produces recommendations mirroring the hurdle race asset management approach. In the authors' opinion, risky asset positions should be maintained during times of a shortfall in wealth. Over time, the shortfall is "cured" by continued exposure to risk. This recommendation contrasts with that of Milevsky and Robinson (2005), who shift the control variable for portfolio sustainability from asset allocation to the timing and magnitude of portfolio withdrawals. We also take note of Browne's (1999) conclusion that the risk (i.e., the amount by which a risky asset position is leveraged) must increase as the time available to correct a shortfall decreases.

The reader is also referred to Gerrard, Hojgaard, and Vigna (2012), who use the term "annuity risk" to characterize the distribution of the present value of an annuity—that is, the risk that lower future interest rates may increase the cost of the annuity to the point where the periodic income is less than the currently achievable annuity income. Wealth falls into a region of "continuation," in which the investor does not annuitize until entering into a "stopping region" when risky assets are then converted into annuity income. The distinction is between an optimal ("propitious") time to exercise the option to annuitize, which is based on financial convenience, and a necessary time to annuitize, which is based on the level of portfolio wealth.

From Fixed Asset Allocations and Bright-Line Spending Rules to Dynamic Risk Monitoring

Depending on the structure of a retirement income risk model, conclusions about cash flow sustainability are usually reached by determining the likelihood that distributions (fixed amounts, percentage of corpus, or "dynamic") can be maintained for either deterministic or stochastic time periods under various asset allocations and longevity assumptions. Sustainability, which is a forward-looking risk metric, is usually quantified by a projection produced by simulation-based models. It differs from the concept of feasibility.

Feasibility is defined as assets exceeding liabilities. Feasibility, or financial solvency, exists when a retirement income portfolio is actuarially solvent—that is, if the current market value of assets equals or exceeds the stochastic present value of the cash flow liabilities. If the value of assets is less than the cost of a lifetime annuity, the targeted periodic withdrawals exceed the resources available to fund them. Under the annuity cost benchmark, such a portfolio violates the feasibility condition. We note that determination of the feasibility of retirement income objectives is not subject to model risk because the determination rests on current observables—annuity cost versus asset value—rather than projections of financial asset returns and investor longevity.

Portfolio insolvency is not the same as portfolio depletion. A portfolio is depleted when it runs out of money. Even a portfolio holding assets with a large current market value, however, is technically insolvent if the asset value is less than the cost of funding future liabilities. Avoiding insolvency may require a different approach to portfolio monitoring and management than one focused exclusively on either maximization of utility or minimization of shortfall probability. The focus on the cost of retirement elevates the importance of monitoring financial resources both in terms of changes in investor needs and circumstances and in terms of the portfolio's financial ability to discharge evolving liabilities. How does the investor assess the portfolio's current financial condition? What is a suitable liability benchmark? What is the likelihood that, absent changes in spending and asset allocation, the investor will have to make future changes in her standard of living? Conditional on a shortfall in future resources, what is the likely range of shortfall magnitude and length of its duration (i.e., the distribution of time alive but broke)? These and other interesting questions constitute the subject matter of recent research into the areas of longevity risk and retirement income planning.

The need for effective portfolio monitoring as a precondition for prudent asset management finds support in Milevsky and Huang (2011). The authors discuss the "rational reaction to a financial shock" over the retirement planning horizon (p. 51). A rule to spend 4% of wealth provides no guidance on updating the spending policy in response to a shock to wealth resulting from a severe market decline. The authors recommend the following steps:

1. Recalibrate the retirement income risk model from time zero but with current wealth equal to the lower amount, and compute a new wealth depletion time equation.

2. Compute the new optimal consumption equation, which yields an amount that differs from the preshock amount.

3. Continue retirement consumption at the new amount.

Milevsky and Huang (2011) provide an example of a 70-year-old retiree experiencing a 31% decrease in portfolio value that necessitates an approximately 20% decrease in consumption. The rational reaction to shocks is "nonlinear and dependent on when the shock is experienced as well as the amount of pre-existing income" (p. 54).[49]

The need for reassessment of investment strategies as a result of market declines also finds expression in a number of essays appearing in 2010, including

- Tahani and Robinson (2010), who say, "Telling a client the standard deviation of returns utterly fails to portray the risk of falling short of a goal" (p. 276);

- Brown and Scahill (2010), who write, "Wealth relative to living expenses is an important factor in the individual's ability to self-insure the longevity risk" (p. 9); and

- Davis (2010), who cautions against trying to develop a set of autopilot portfolio distribution rules: "Rather than trying to develop such a mechanical rule for time-varying parameters, it may make more sense for investors (and their advisers) to periodically review the appropriateness of current parameter values. This would allow the individual's current circumstances to be factored into the decision" (p. 19).

What Does Retirement Cost? An Annuity Benchmark

Many retirement income models peg the cost of retirement as the SPV of the liabilities—income, gift, and bequest—that the portfolio must fund. Indeed, the feasibility condition, which motivates ongoing tracking of solvency status, requires that the current market value of assets equal or exceed the liability's SPV.

Additionally, the following portfolio evaluation approaches are commonly encountered within the literature:

- A backtest of historical returns to determine suitable combinations of spending rules and asset allocation policies

---

[49]Waring and Siegel (2015) recommend something similar, except that consumption adjusts linearly and one-for-one with changes in portfolio value caused by market movements. They assert that if the investor finds such consumption adjustments too jarring, that is *prima facie* evidence that he is taking too much investment risk and should ratchet risk down accordingly.

- A bootstrapped reshuffling of historical returns

- A Monte Carlo simulation of predetermined parameter values to evaluate how various allocations can withstand the stress of portfolio withdrawals

Horizon estimates can be simplistic (e.g., preset, such as 30 years, or a time horizon reflecting life expectancy for the general population or a segment of it). Life expectancy–based time horizons are simplistic because they ignore the entire right half of the distribution: Suppose the investor lives beyond the expected amount of time. What is he or she supposed to live on?

Given the empirical fact that, until recently, the US S&P 500 Index has regularly outperformed bond indexes over periods greater than 10 years, many studies recommend maintaining an equity position greater than that suggested by the financial planning rule of 100 minus current age. Prior to the 2008–09 global financial crisis, an often-heard recommendation was "stocks for the long run." The precipitous drop in stock values, however, underscored the fact that a retired investor's standard of living depends on actual, rather than expected, return. Given the uncertainty in mean and variance parameters, how confident can the long-term investor be with analytical approximation formulas, empirical backtests, or simulation outputs that promote the belief that stocks always save the day—especially when retirement distributions create path dependencies (sequence risk)? Questions of (1) a credible measure of retirement's true cost and (2) a credible methodology to assess whether the portfolio owns sufficient assets to cover the cost assume greater urgency post-recession.

For example, Milevsky (2011) contends that an immediate annuity is the best measure of retirement cost. Milevsky insists that the cost of providing adequate retirement income is not magically reduced by loading a portfolio with higher expected return assets: "Enter the retirement planning software used by confused—or unscrupulous—financial advisers and they seem to offer a better and more soothing answer. If you invest more aggressively then you do not have to use the small, pathetic and depressing 1.5% real return" (p. 3). However, this is a mirage—"You cannot tweak expected return (a.k.a. asset allocations) assumptions until you get the numbers that you like" (p. 4). Stock returns are uncertain and "pricing" the cost of retirement based on expected stock returns is the equivalent of making a bet: "Assuming a more aggressive rate of return. . . and then claiming that retirement has suddenly become 'cheaper' is a dangerous fallacy that will end up costing many retirees quite dearly" (p. 5). Milevsky asserts, "The annuity price is actually a market signal of what retirement really costs" (p. 5).

Although financial economists had long recognized the importance of portfolio monitoring and surveillance policy for prudent asset management, researchers began to pose questions about the risk metrics on which such a policy should focus. What are the best metrics for assessing portfolio risk, and what are the asset management elections available to investors concerned with a financially successful retirement? Robinson and Tahani (2010) combine risk metrics—shortfall risk plus feasibility—to generate insights into retirement consumption choices. The authors note, "Retirees can and often do adjust their spending to some extent to respond to changes in their endowment due to higher or lower than expected investment returns" (p. 188).

Robinson and Tahani (2010) argue that spending adjustments are the most important factor in reducing the risk of shortfall. They observe that, rather than a fixed consumption policy, retirement spending often follows a declining pattern. The sustainability of the portfolio depends on both the initial endowment and the spending pattern that unfolds over the retiree's lifespan. The authors state that most research on portfolio sustainability either presents a series of *ad hoc* rules for spending change or assumes a constant amount of real consumption. By contrast, Robinson and Tahani treat consumption as a stochastic variable with a drift component of $-\alpha$ and a volatility of β (a geometric Brownian motion process). When α is a positive number, the $-\alpha$ drift represents an exponential decline in consumption. Further, their retirement income risk model correlates consumption to the portfolio's real return, thus making consumption stochastic. When the SPV of consumption is greater than portfolio value (wealth), there is a positive probability of ruin. They conclude, "The most significant effect on probability of shortfall . . . is the different patterns of consumption" (p. 193). As previously noted, Blanchett (2014) estimates retirement cost given empirical spending patterns of retired investors.

An infrequently cited, but significant, article by Jones (2000) also calls into question the use of an annuity as a valid benchmark for calculating the total cost of retirement. An annuity is a mortality-adjusted present value cost for predetermined periodic cash flows. But many retirement income needs cannot be predetermined. Jones states: "A retirement income determined so that the actuarial present value of the income equals the actuarial present value of the costs will likely not provide the retiree with adequate security, since there may be a high probability that the income will be inadequate. To help determine a more appropriate income, it is useful to know the distribution of the 'adequate income amount,' that is, the income that, if paid through the lifetime of the retiree, has the same present value as the costs" (p. 84).

To determine the distribution, Jones simulates a large number of possible health state transition processes, calculates the amount of "adequate income" for each trial, and ranks the outcomes. Depending on the number, magnitude, length, and sequence of less-than-optimal health states—as well as transitions back to improved health states—Jones can generate histograms of retirement cash needs.

The model incorporates four states—active, frail, disabled, and dead—with a cost structure associated with each state. Only certain transition sequences are permitted; it is rare to find a transition from death. Many investors die without experiencing significant expenses for frailty, sickness, or disability. However, the distribution of costs, which quantifies the financial risk faced by retirees for health care expenses, exhibits a strong right skew. The pattern of income needs faced by retirees varies considerably: "The level income that has the same actuarial present value as the costs may not provide adequate security. It is, therefore, of interest to examine the distribution of the adequate level income. This is the level income that has the same present value as the costs given the outcome of the multistate process" (Jones 2000, p. 85).

Jones's (2000) study stresses the importance of modeling the liabilities as stochastic rather than deterministic variables. And by presenting a multistate model of a Markov transition process wherein the investor's spending needs are, in part, a function of his health state, Jones provides important guidance to retirement income risk model builders. Jones directs the model builder's attention to a concept that might best be termed the "sequence risk" of health care costs. It is not so much the average cost or the total aggregate cost that produces a credible retirement income risk model. Rather, it is the timing and amount of costs in retirement that may determine portfolio adequacy.

In contrast to Robinson and Tahani (2010), Li (2008) argues the importance of asset allocation. Li's argument, however, emerges from a different context. The author is interested in exploring the future distribution of annuity costs and in comparing this distribution with the distribution of returns achievable by self-annuitizing with various portfolio asset weightings. Li's study is of great interest in that it is one of the few that explores, in depth, the distribution of the present value of a life annuity under stochastic interest rates and mortality. Assuming that current wealth permits the purchase of an annuity providing sufficient periodic consumption (i.e., current wealth ≥ PV annuity), then annuitization is a risk-free strategy in terms of locking in a nominal consumption floor. Electing a self-annuitization strategy, by contrast, carries a positive probability of ruin. Thus, the PV of an annuity is an appropriate standard for measuring the risks of self-annuitization.

Li (2008) provides an intellectual underpinning for a credible retirement portfolio monitoring and surveillance methodology. The study makes the case that the best measure of self-annuitization risk is the uncertainty surrounding a portfolio's ability to maintain a value equal to or greater than the present value of an annuity. The risk of continuing to manage a risky-asset portfolio in the hope that it will produce wealth sufficient to buy an annuity that generates higher future income is, in part, a function of the distribution of future annuity costs.

The "present value of an annuity" is defined in Li (2008) as the present value of the cost of funding lifetime retirement obligations either through direct purchase of an annuity contract or through a strategy of self-annuitization. Thus, "annuity" can, depending on the context, refer to a contract offered by an insurance company or a sum of money necessary to provide withdrawals from an investment portfolio. The annuity contract benefits the retiree because of its embedded mortality longevity-risk protection; the risky-asset portfolio benefits the retiree because of its expected risk premium. Assuming a wealth-to-consumption ratio (w/k) that must finance constant lifetime consumption $(k,$ where k matches the withdrawal amount provided by a commercial annuity), the probability of ruin (portfolio depletion) is the likelihood that the PV of lifetime consumption exceeds the PV of the annuity alternative.

Li's (2008) procedures for generating the interest rates required to price annuity contracts in the future years employs an Ornstein–Uhlenbeck (OU) process for generating stochastic interest rate paths. OU is a mean-reverting process where the instantaneous change in the interest rate is a differential equation with terms for (1) a coefficient of reversion, (2) the magnitude of difference between current and long-term average interest rates, and (3) a diffusion coefficient (σ) applied to a standard Brownian-motion process. An OU process allows for auto-correlation in both the drift and diffusion terms. As the OU process unfolds over time, the rate of return accumulation function is the integration from time zero to time t of the investment returns. The return accumulation function $[Y(t)]$ is normally distributed, and the present value of the accumulation function is lognormally distributed. Finally, the PV of the annuity function is the standard actuarial annuity pricing formula with its terms adjusted for uncertainty in both life expectancy and the interest rate. In continuous-time finance, the expected price of a whole life annuity (the first moment) is $\int_0^\infty E\left[e^{-Y(t)}\right]_t P_x \times dt$. The discrete-time equivalent uses sums rather than the integral, with the limiting upper bound being the oldest age in the mortality table. Li calculates the first four moments of the PV annuity function.

The key element for an effective retirement income portfolio monitoring system lies in estimation of the distribution of the present value of an annuity. Li (2008) employs three methods to calculate this distribution: (1) a recursive formula (using trapezoidal numerical integration), (2) fitting the moments to known distributions (best fit = reciprocal gamma distribution), and (3) simulation under an OU process. The simulation and recursion results are close; the gamma distribution has a poor left-tail fit, especially for high-volatility parameters. Li concludes that the choice of asset allocation is the single most important factor affecting the probability of ruin under a measure that uses the annuity payout as the benchmark for the withdrawal amount.

We also call attention to Shankar (2009) as an example of establishing a retirement cost benchmark based on combinations of TIPS (Treasury Inflation-Protected Securities) and annuities. In this case, the author claims that alternative investment strategies must be evaluated not in terms of their expected future returns or their shortfall probability under specific withdrawal strategies but, rather, relative to a risk-free benchmark matching the investor's minimum target income. After stating that an annuity is the only instrument that eliminates the possibility of ruin, the author proposes an inflation-protected retirement annuity (IPRA) strategy unfolding in two stages:

1. For the initial stage, TIPS are purchased until a target age is reached (e.g., age 80). The TIPS portfolio is depleted at this time.

2. At the time of the TIPS portfolio purchase, a premium is paid to buy a deferred annuity that pays out only in the event that the investor survives stage one. For surviving investors, the annuity pays a constant-dollar ("real," not nominal) benefit for life. A constant-dollar annuity option, however, is not widely offered in the marketplace, and investors might need to adjust the future annuity payout to reflect the erosion of nominal payouts over time.

Shankar's (2009) recommendations parallel those made by Scott (2008) and by Sexauer and Siegel (2013). The importance of an annuity benchmark increases as authors begin to rethink the appropriate set of risk metrics. We cover this topic in the next section.

New Characterizations of Risk Metrics

Initially, many retirement income models tested primarily for shortfalls in terminal wealth under various predetermined spending policies. Commentators often advocate a high portfolio weight in equity under the assumption that assets with a high expected return can best mitigate longevity risk. The prescription to (1) hold stocks, (2) stay the course, and (3) keep consumption low comes primarily from a focus on a terminal wealth shortfall risk metric (e.g., a safe retirement portfolio should be expected to last 30 or more years so that it can provide income to a healthy 65-year-old retiree). The implication is that the prescription to hold a large equity weight is prudent because portfolios tilted toward fixed income present an unacceptably high risk of ruin.

Some recent modeling efforts focus both on terminal wealth—wealth remaining after a preset number of years or wealth remaining at the end of the investor's life—and on the periodic income available to support consumption targets. When the retirement risk model focuses primarily on terminal wealth, the control variable is spending. Unfortunately, this approach does not comport well with the way many retired investors deal with risk—especially in light of the need to support a threshold standard of living. This section provides a brief review of an expanded set of risk metrics. It offers examples of models designed to provide insight into the wealth versus consumption trade-offs central to prudent retirement portfolio monitoring and management.

The importance of providing adequate periodic income augments the importance of annuities in retirement portfolio modeling and monitoring. The enhanced role that annuities play in the discussion reflects recent recommendations for establishing actuarial guidelines—in some models, the guidelines assume the status of a benchmark—both (1) for assessing the portfolio's financial condition relative to outstanding income, gift, and bequest objectives and (2) for considering acquisition of an annuity to provide future income through contractual rather than investment means.

Terminal Wealth vs. Consumption Variance. Rather than focusing exclusively on the probability of a shortfall in terminal wealth, Williams and Finke (2011) test portfolio design and consumption policy under the assumption that "the appropriate portfolio allocation in retirement is the one that minimizes consumption variance given the chosen withdrawal rate" (p. 36). A high withdrawal rate increases the probability that the portfolio will run out of money with the result that the client must live only on "nonportfolio income." The authors acknowledge that "the more that is consumed from portfolio withdrawals in retirement, the higher the variance due to increased shortfall risk" (p. 37). The authors advocate, however, for "a more holistic approach to distribution planning [which] would attempt to design a distribution strategy that optimizes consumption given the strategy's shortfall risk and client's aversion to [income] variance" rather than defaulting to an exclusive use of a shortfall risk metric (p. 37). Their retirement income risk model assumes that the investor has funds outside of the portfolio (e.g., Social Security and other pension wealth), so that portfolio depletion is not catastrophic. Their model incorporates the CRRA form of the utility function.

In contrast to studies that emphasize a host of terminal wealth risk metrics—a ratio of ending wealth to initial wealth, nominal or constant-dollar remaining wealth, and so forth—Williams and Finke (2011) point out that longevity risk may result in a time-preference discounting rate that differs from the general risk-free rate: "A utility maximizer will discount future consumption based on the probability of being alive for each year in the future. If the discount rate is 4% per year, the expected utility from consumption at age 82 will be only approximately half the utility from consumption at age 65. In order to maximize expected lifetime utility then, a retiree would consume more in the early years of retirement and less in the later years when the probability of being alive is lower" (p. 39).

Furthermore, Williams and Finke (2011) write: "A person might be incented to defer some consumption until a later time if the expected return were high enough. Both the discount and expected return rates are inversely related to risk aversion. A person with a high RRA [relative risk aversion] will have a relatively low expected rate of return due to conservative portfolio choice but will also not discount future consumption much because he is not willing to accept much variability in consumption. If these rates are equal, then holding real consumption constant is utility maximizing" (p. 40).

The authors test allocations and withdrawal rates for retirees with differing levels of secure, nonportfolio-related income. Portfolio depletion results in a "bad" economic state in which consumption depends only on nonportfolio income. "For each withdrawal rate chosen," the authors write, "the optimal portfolio allocation is the one that is expected to minimize the percentage of bad years. . . or (minimize) variance of consumption for that withdrawal rate" (p. 43).

Shortfall Risk in Consumption vs. Shortfall Risk in Wealth. A study of particular relevance is Pang (2012). He attempts to identify the best combination of mutual funds and single premium immediate annuities during retirement. Pang employs a vector autoregressive model using the S&P 500 return, 10-year government bond total return, and 90-day T-bill return based on 1962–2009 quarterly data. Economic shocks are incorporated based on a model developed by Barro (2009). Insurance carriers are assumed to fail with an annual probability of 0.15%. The discount rate for annuity pricing is based on the yields on 10-year US Treasury bonds. Annuity pricing uses the annuitant population mortality table with an additional load of 10% to cover administration and marketing costs. Survival of retirees, however, is simulated using general population unisex mortality tables.

Pang (2012) writes: "The success criterion for the strategy search is to minimize the shortfall risk, which is defined as a weighted probability of real income and wealth balances falling below certain thresholds, in a stochastic model. The objective somewhat departs from the conventional analytical assumption that investors maximize their expected utility over consumption and bequests" (p. 163).

59

Consumption shortfall is defined as a withdrawal that falls below a pre-established threshold amount. A shortfall in wealth is defined as lacking sufficient funds to cover uninsured contingencies or to leave a targeted level of bequests. In the Pang (2012) model, mitigation of consumption shortfall risk competes with mitigation of wealth shortfall risk.

The model incorporates the effects of multiple factors, including minimum threshold income requirements, investment fees, and expenses. His research touches on critical trade-offs between investment and actuarial approaches to generating adequate lifetime income. Mutual fund investment enables the retiree to improve the budget constraint if returns are good but exposes the investor to significant consumption declines if returns are poor. Annuity purchases in low interest rate environments also constitute a significant risk. However, delaying an annuity purchase may risk further losses in the mutual fund portfolio, with the result that the investor may lack sufficient funds to purchase the desired amount of future annuity income. The risks and benefits of asset management elections are more fully highlighted by such complex and realistic models. The exemplification and quantification of these options within retirement income risk models are fast becoming a prerequisite to effective portfolio management.

Shortfall Risk in Terminal Wealth vs. Maximization of Lifetime Income Opportunities. Closely related to the bequest versus income trade-off is an assessment of retirement fund strategies in terms of lost opportunity costs. The idea is a development of the portfolio preferencing criteria that we discussed in the review of Gerrard et al. (2004). This line of research views a strategy designed to enhance portfolio sustainability by piling up large amounts of future wealth, absent a bequest motive, as suboptimal because it diminishes opportunities for lifetime consumption. The issue is, of course, a variation on the question of lifetime consumption versus terminal wealth shortfall metrics.

Consider, for example, Sexauer, Peskin, and Cassidy (2012). The authors point out: "Most of the academic research with respect to retirement strategies has focused on the right tail, where the concern is outliving one's assets. In our study, we attempted to bring much-needed attention to the left tail, where the concern is getting as much income as possible while a large majority of retirees are still alive" (p. 77). The authors suggest creating a benchmark to evaluate the success of a retirement income investment strategy. In this case, the benchmark consists of a suitable combination of TIPS and an ALDA—advanced life deferred annuity. The benchmark is investable: A retiree can implement this two-asset portfolio, and the spendable income that it generates measures how well an investment program designed to beat the benchmark is actually performing.

Although Sexauer et al. (2012) acknowledge that the best benchmark is an inflation-adjusted immediate annuity, they reject an annuity as a suitable performance evaluation benchmark: "The cash flows from a real, immediate life annuity are unsuitable as a general benchmark for asset decumulation because the illiquidity of such a strategy is so burdensome that almost no one uses it" (p. 74). Their rejection of an SPIA as a *performance benchmark*, however, does not imply that an SPIA is not a valid measure of the *cost* of retirement—that is, the current market value of the stochastic present value of retirement cash flow liabilities. The distinction is between a performance evaluation benchmark and a portfolio solvency benchmark. Additional discussion of appropriate retirement performance benchmarks is found in Cassidy, Peskin, Siegel, and Sexauer (2013).

Conditional vs. Unconditional Shortfall Risk. Finke, Pfau, and Williams (2012) develop a model designed to identify solution paths based on expected utility. The model employs a bootstrap methodology, consists of a two asset class portfolio, incorporates the CRRA form of the utility function, and further assumes that the investor has guaranteed nonportfolio income. The authors criticize the use of a shortfall risk metric, but the guaranteed "pension" income stream allows them to bypass—almost too conveniently— many difficulties that flow from their model's oversimplified assumptions.

Finke et al.'s (2012) critique of the shortfall risk metric, however, is germane.[50] They assert that shortfall risk analysis may not be the best preferencing criterion for selecting a retirement income strategy:

> By emphasizing a portfolio's ability to withstand a 30- or 40-year retirement, we ignore the fact that at age 65 the probability of either spouse being alive by age 95 is only 18%. If we strive for a 90% confidence level that the portfolio will provide a constant real income stream for a least 30 years, this means that we are planning for an eventuality that is only likely to occur 1.8% of the time. And even that figure assumes that clients are unable to make adjustments to their spending later in retirement. So by relying on standard historical or Monte Carlo simulations to determine a safe withdrawal rate, clients may be unduly sacrificing much of their desired lifestyle early in retirement. The failure to include a client's willingness to adjust is an important shortfall of the shortfall literature. A common thread in the analysis is that all failures are counted the same, without regard to when the failure occurred or what percentage of the client's stated aggregate spending goal was funded. Such an all-or-nothing approach to retirement simulation is inconsistent with the way trade-offs are framed in retirement. (p. 44)

---

[50]We note that a similar—albeit more technical and mathematically elegant—critique of unconditional shortfall as a measure of risk is found in Albrecht and Maurer (2001). This article, however, is not often cited in the literature because it deals with data from the German stock and bond markets.

It is not enough, then, for a retiree to know that a shortfall might take place. The magnitude of the shortfall is also of importance—especially if the retiree has resources beyond the financial portfolio. This implies, of course, that any portfolio monitoring and evaluation system incorporating a shortfall risk metric must account for both the probability of the failure as well as its magnitude should the failure occur. Interestingly, for many values of the CRRA risk aversion coefficient, the Finke et al. (2012) model identifies an optimal withdrawal rate and asset allocation strategy that does not minimize shortfall risk. In fact, in this model, the investor elects portfolio management strategies, under a utility-based preferencing metric, that have a relatively high likelihood of depleting the portfolio during the life of the retired investor.

Shortfall Risk and High Risk Aversion vs. Fisher Utility and High Subjective Discounting. Milevsky (2012) discusses Irving Fisher's viewpoint on the utility of retirement consumption. Determination of the optimal consumption level includes factors for (1) investor risk aversion, (2) subjective discounting of the utility of future consumption (e.g., a preference for income in early retirement, assuming good health and the capacity to enjoy leisure activities), and (3) longevity expectations. In terms of setting a retirement income budget, the risk aversion factor reflects a concern with outliving financial resources. A high coefficient of risk aversion, or a low elasticity of intertemporal substitution, leads to a conservative spending rate in early retirement. Conversely, a high subjective preference rate discounts the value of future income and leads to higher spending during early retirement. This tug of war is, of course, one aspect of the general risk–reward trade-off faced by retired investors.

Milevsky states: "Irving Fisher the economist was the first to properly formulate how *rational consumers* should adjust their consumption spending over time. This is the intertemporal aspect of economic tradeoffs" (p. 78). Data from the US Department of Labor suggest that "by 65, retirees are spending between 50% and 70% of what they did at 50. And, by 80 it has dropped to under 60%" (p. 83). Milevsky quotes from Fisher (1930): "Uncertainty of human life increases the rate of preference for present over future income for many people" (Milevsky, p. 91). Investors exhibiting Fisher utility prefer to spend and enjoy scarce resources today rather than husband them against a remote contingent probability that they might be needed at an advanced age. Milevsky also notes that Yaari (1965) translates Fisher's view of investor utility into a mathematical expression suitable for life-cycle modeling.

The Fisher view of retirement income utility has several implications. Seemingly, it stands in an uncomfortable relationship with a "budgetary-certainty" approach. Many retirees derive satisfaction from knowing that their portfolio can produce a steady monthly constant-dollar income. Indeed, throughout much of this literature review, we comment on retirement income risk models that emphasize achievement of a sustainable *threshold* income in each period. The threshold represents the lower boundary of income that is acceptable to the retiree.[51] The budget goal is akin to the "hurdle race problem" discussed in the previously cited article by Vanduffel et al. (2003). Some models assume a HARA or a state-preference utility function, the violation of which, given the retired investor's preferences and constraints, generates disutility. In these models, maximization of additive utility across all states gives way to achieving, at least, a positive utility hurdle in each state. Furthermore, the introduction of an income threshold creates the conditions under which calculation of the free boundary—the portfolio's feasibility condition—is both necessary and possible, which, in turn, promotes the creation of risk models that ensure compatibility between a utility-based portfolio preferencing system and a system based on safety-first or shortfall risk metrics.

Additionally, we note a predilection by some retired investors to backload their retirement income spending policy—for example, when in previous generations, family members faced significant end-of-life costs or when there is a significant age difference between spouses. Such a spending preference turns the Fisher optimal retirement consumption path on its head. It is further proof that preset rules, combinations of rules, and one-size-fits-all bright-line spending policies are problematic.

The Gordon Pye Model: Retirement Planning with Scarce Resources

In 2012, Gordon Pye, former University of California, Berkeley, finance professor, published a book on retirement income strategies for investors owning modest-sized portfolios. His premise is that many, if not most, retired investors lack sufficient capital to finance sustainable lifetime income at a level that can permanently preserve their prior standard of living. Additionally, many do not have the option to continue in their jobs past normal retirement age. Given the economic reality that these retirees face, "the key question in spending retirement assets [is] not achieving sustainable withdrawals, but when to retrench" (p. xv). There is no doubt that spending cuts must occur. However, if the initial cut in spending is so great that it forces an unacceptably high level of immediate economic pain, then a more gradual schedule of reductions may be the preferred alternative provided that the reductions do not result in unacceptably low future withdrawals.

---

[51]Of course, any budget must provide funds at a minimum subsistence level.

Pye (2012) advances the following argument: "The initial withdrawal should be the one required to provide the prior or desired standard of living subject to a limit. That limit should be the largest withdrawal that could be made without increasing too much the risk of low withdrawals later in retirement. Moreover, this limit should be based on the discount rate that gives the best results in a series of simulated withdrawals" (p. xv). The discount rate that gives the best results (i.e., balancing sufficient current income against the probability-adjusted likelihood of lower future cash flow) is the retrenchment discount rate, the application of which is the retrenchment rule. Pye's retirement withdrawal strategy is aimed at retirees who exhibit a strong preference to maintain their current standard of living (i.e., habit utility) but who own resources insufficient to support the required cash flows throughout long planning horizons: "The present value of the withdrawals required to sustain their existing standard of living exceeds the value of their initial investment. Thus, these retirees will have to retrench" (p. 269). Classic life-cycle utility-based models tell us that the investor seeks to optimize utility by following a smoothed consumption path. A drastic reduction in spending at the moment of retirement, however, creates an unacceptable path discontinuity.

Given Pye's (2012) premise, following the 4% initial withdrawal strategy will not work for many retirees because "many individuals have to begin retirement without having saved nearly enough to cover essential expenses with a 4% withdrawal" (p. 1). Although the 4% rule often forces draconian budget reductions, Pye notes that such reductions may prove unnecessary if (1) initial investment returns are above expectation or (2) the investor suffers a health decline that adversely affects longevity expectations.[52]

Pye (2012) illustrates the difficulties with the 4% rule. He conducts two tests assuming an annually rebalanced portfolio of 75% S&P 500 and 25% intermediate US government bonds. The first test applies the 4% rule to a 65-year-old investor, in good health, beginning retirement in 1991. Despite the bear markets in stocks both early and late in the first decade of the 21st century, the retiree is able to sustain a 7.5% withdrawal rate through 2010—the time of the book's composition. However, if the hypothetical retirement starts in 1966, an initial withdrawal strategy of 7.5% would have required gradual reductions in withdrawals to avoid portfolio depletion. By 1982, the retiree can withdraw only 2.1% of the initial portfolio value. As it turns out, 1966 was the worst year to retire of all years since 1926. This conclusion may strike some readers as ironic because the stock market was high in 1966, a good time to sell, but subsequent real returns were very poor, causing the distressing result that Pye found. By contrast, 1991 was the most favorable year for retirement.

---

[52]Pye's observations are variations on the theme presented by Dus, Maurer, and Mitchell (2005).

Pye's (2012) point is this: Following the 4% rule would result in a significant and unnecessary permanent reduction in income for the 1991 retirees. For 1966 retirees, the 4% rule would have curtailed early retirement income substantially (from 7.5% to 4.0% of initial portfolio value) and would nevertheless have fully depleted the portfolio by 1996 (30 years). He writes: "Those who withdrew 7.5% in 1966 eventually had to retrench somewhat more. But they had 10 years (before they hit the 4% withdrawal target level) over which to plan and make these adjustments. . . . Also, with good health, and perhaps some pent-up enthusiasm for activities such as travel, increments of spending early in retirement are likely to provide more satisfaction than equal increments later on" (p. 6). The bottom line is that the 4% rule mandates an immediate and substantial reduction in many retirees' standard of living. Drawing on observations similar to those made by Irving Fisher, Pye states, "The Retrenchment Rule weighs whether this immediate pain is justified given that the future funds provided may turn out to never be needed" (p. 1).[53] The retrenchment rule requires a more modest type of glide path reduction, and of crucial importance is that this reduction is implemented only if an unfavorable sequence of returns unfolds.

Clearly, a primary control variable for Pye's (2012) version of dynamic asset management is the withdrawal amount. Examination of all historical periods since 1926 reveals that withdrawals beginning at the 7.5% rate stay above the 4% rate in 70% of the cases. Cuts should be made when the withdrawal rate is unsustainable. But retirees do not know *ex ante* the future sequence of returns, inflation rates, or health changes that they will face. Therefore, according to Pye, the utility-maximizing retiree avoids making immediate and economically painful cuts when such cuts may, in fact, prove unnecessary. Any retiree with a positive time preference for consumption will wish to avoid painful retrenchment forced on him at the beginning of his retirement by a 4% withdrawal rule.

Pye's (2012) argument for beginning initial consumption in retirement at a relatively high level seems to run counter to recommendations made by commentators using a shortfall or risk-of-ruin portfolio monitoring metric, but it does not. Pye's argument is to cut back when necessary, cut back as gradually as possible to preserve a smoothed consumption path, and make sure that the portfolio does not outlive the investor. Fundamentally, Pye asks the investor to make deliberate, well-considered asset management decisions rather than defaulting to a fixed, autopilot withdrawal rule designed to protect the portfolio from low-probability events. As such, Pye's suggestions conform both to the classical utility-based approach to retirement portfolio management and to the shortfall avoidance approach.

---

[53]Fisher is not mentioned in Pye (2012).

The following paragraph, for example, reveals Pye's (2012) academic grounding in life-cycle utility modeling:

> Future investment withdrawals of the same real value are worth less the further in the future they are expected to occur. One reason is that it becomes increasingly less likely that retirees will survive that long. Another is that many have pent-up plans for activities after they retire such as travel, but these desires become satisfied. Also, later on withdrawals of the same real value are likely to provide less satisfaction as lifestyles slow and mobility declines even for those who remain in as good health as can be expected. To reflect this decreasing value the Retrenchment Rule discounts future withdrawals by a constant rate of interest for each year in the future until they will be made. The value of this discount rate is selected by simulating the use of the rule with different rates over a hypothetical retirement period. This is to see which rate gives the best performance. The discount rate selected is called the Retrenchment Discount Rate, or RDR. (p. 12)

However, Pye (2012) also recognizes that retired investors are averse to the risk of outliving financial resources. Although Pye does not use the term "feasibility condition" when discussing decumulation strategies, he advances an argument that is compatible with this concept:

> To reflect their declining value future withdrawals are discounted by a constant rate of interest for each year in the future until they occur. This discounting gives the present value of a future withdrawal based on the discount rate that has been used. Adding up these discounted values for each of the withdrawals gives the present value of the stream. This is the present value of the future withdrawals in real terms needed to provide the existing standard of living. The present value of the funds available to make these withdrawals is the current value of the investment portfolio. Suppose the present value of the stream of withdrawals required to provide the existing standard of living is less than the value of the portfolio. Then retrenchment is not required. . . . There are sufficient funds to provide the existing standard of living in the future. On the other hand, suppose that the present value of the stream to provide the existing standard of living exceeds the value of the portfolio. Then retrenchment is required. (p. 21)

This language puts Pye (2012) close to the school of retirement portfolio management that focuses primarily on period-by-period income sustainability, and it conforms to a free boundary/portfolio solvency monitoring approach.

A key issue is how to determine the appropriate discount rate. The best discount rate, according to Pye (2012), is the RDR, and this rate is determined by calculating the present value of the stream of future withdrawals required to provide a given standard of living—the desired discount rate—limited, in turn, by the discount rate that gives the "best" results. "Best" here is defined as the most appropriate trade-off between current cash flows and possible lower future cash flows across the distribution of simulated results.[54] Simulations assume a maximum lifespan of age 110.

For example, suppose that a retired investor in good health requires an initial withdrawal rate of 8% from her modest-sized portfolio. At this rate, she can avoid making a painful cut in her standard of living. If the RDR with the best trade-off between current cash flow adequacy and the likelihood of future painful income reductions is 6%, however, then some immediate retrenchment must occur. Pye writes: "Suppose that the value of the investment is 100 so that the required withdrawal is 8. Input $n = 45$ $(110 - 65 = 45)$, $I = 6.0$, $PMT = 8$, and $FV = 0$. Calculate the present value of this stream getting 131.1, which exceeds the value of the investment of 100. . . . When the withdrawals have declined from 8 to 6.1 their present value has fallen to 100. As this is the value of the portfolio this withdrawal is allowed. It is the largest withdrawal allowed by the Retrenchment Rule with a discount rate of 0.06" (p. 25). Another way of looking at this calculation is that "it is the largest fixed annuity that can be obtained each year from the investment for the longest that the retiree might live. This is when the investment earns a return equal to the assumed discount rate of 0.06. A larger stream of withdrawals than this annuity will have a present value that exceeds the value of the investment and will require retrenchment" (p. 25).

It is worth noting that the discount rate (RDR) for this hypothetical annuity is not derived from the current term structure of interest rates. Neither is it the expected portfolio rate of return. Rather, it is a discount rate derived from a process of trial and error over the entire distribution of simulated portfolio returns.

The following is how Pye's (2012) example plays out in a dynamic portfolio monitoring and withdrawal setting:

> For making the simulations it is assumed that 6.1% is withdrawn at the beginning of the year and spent over the year. Another withdrawal is not made until the beginning of the following year. Suppose the real return

---

[54]Pye's (2012) discount rate approach is, in some respects, the opposite side of the coin from the "equivalent payment value" developed by Hughen, Laatsch, and Klein (2002). The equivalent payment value expresses terminal wealth in terms of the extra periodic payment that could have been received throughout the planning horizon. It is "calculated using an interest rate equal to the total return on equity over the particular time period" (Hughen et al. 2002, p. 363). This value is then expressed as a percentage of the initial portfolio value. Assume a $1 million portfolio with terminal wealth of $1.4 million. Total annual return on equity for a 20-year period is 10%. If this had been converted into a nominal annual payment, the amount of extra yearly income would be $24,443. As a percentage of initial portfolio value, terminal wealth was sufficient to support a 2.4% increase in the nominal withdrawal rate. Given that the equivalent payment value is a backward-looking calculation, it has limited use in a portfolio monitoring system.

on the portfolio over the coming year is 3%. The value of the portfolio at the beginning of the following year before a withdrawal is made is then (100 − 6.1)(1.03), or 96.72. This is in real terms because the return of 3% is in real terms. The $96.72 portfolio value is 96.72% of the initial investment because the initial investment is equal to $100.

The Retrenchment Rule is now applied just as it was initially to get the next withdrawal. All of the inputs have changed, however, except that the discount rate is still 6%. To calculate the largest allowed withdrawal, the user inputs $n = 44$, $PV = 96.72$, $i = 6\%$, and $FV = 0$. Calculate PMT getting $5.90 (that is, 5.9% of $100) as the largest withdrawal allowed by the Retrenchment Rule.

As $6.10 must be withdrawn to sustain the prior standard of living, some retrenchment is required. Suppose that a severe bear market occurs over the coming year and that the real return is −25% instead of +3%. In this case the value of the investment at the beginning of the following year is (100 − 6.1)(0.75), or $70.42. Calculating PMT, in this case the largest allowed withdrawal is $4.30. Now a major retrenchment is required. The withdrawal must be reduced from $6.10 to $4.30.

Suppose only $4.00 had been withdrawn initially instead of $6.10. In this case a major retrenchment is required initially, but no retrenchment is necessary at the beginning of the following year. The value of the investment is now (100 − 4.0)(0.75), or $72.00. But this is only slightly higher than the $70.42 obtained with the $6.10 withdrawal. Thus, suppose a severe bear market occurs in the coming year. It then makes little difference if the Retrenchment Rule is used with a 6% discount rate or there is a 4% withdrawal. The advantage of the higher withdrawal is the very strong chance that a much better return will be earned over the coming year. In this event major retrenchment may never be necessary. . . . If only 4% is withdrawn initially a major retrenchment occurs for sure immediately. (p. 26)

In the Pye (2012) method, portfolio management decisions are based not on an expected future return but on current observables—age and portfolio value. The extreme conservatism of calculating the applicable planning horizon based on the maximum age in the mortality table balances the extreme liberalism of higher initial withdrawal rates. This is a key point of differentiation between Pye's portfolio monitoring and evaluation method and that of others. It is almost as if Pye is betting that the two error terms—longevity span and withdrawal amounts in excess of what can be sustained under all historical conditions—will cancel each other out, thus leaving the investor with the expectation of an adequate retirement income. By contrast, alternative monitoring and portfolio evaluation approaches, using an annuity benchmark, directly incorporate the force of mortality and the term structure of interest rates via the annuity pricing factor.

The process of recalculating the allowable withdrawal amount, including simulation of the distribution of future returns and recalculation of the most appropriate discount rate, continues each year through a maximum age of 109. Pye states: "Suppose next that the discount rate is 0.08 instead of 0.06. In this case the largest allowed initial withdrawal is the value of the annuity obtained when the investment earns a return of 0.08 instead of 0.06. The largest allowed initial withdrawal in this case rises from 6.1 to 7.6%. If the required withdrawal to avoid initial retrenchment is still 8% the initial withdrawal increases to 7.6%" (p. 28). This is the limit imposed by the annuity calculation for $n = 45$ (the number of years from age 65 to 109) and $FV = 0$ (where FV represents the Future Value key on a financial calculator). If a major health crisis occurs, planning over the long horizon may be sufficiently conservative so that funds will be available to provide the needed liquidity. Thus, Pye views the lack of precision in his monitoring system as a virtue: Overstating the probability of a long lifespan is equivalent to building in a reserve in the event that expected longevity is cut short by health changes.

The gist of Pye's (2012) observations is that a higher discount rate (i.e., RDR) provides higher withdrawals early in retirement. However, the high withdrawals may deplete the portfolio more rapidly than a withdrawal strategy calculated under a lower RDR. Selection of a high RDR results in a higher probability of future retirement retrenchment. Assuming a normal return distribution with stocks having an expected return of 7% and a standard deviation of 18, all retirees will select a discount rate of 8% because the expected withdrawals at this rate are higher than those for any lower RDR. Thus, 8% exhibits a property of dominance at each age. For example, a discount rate of 10% offers a higher probability of a lower withdrawal at age 90 than does an RDR of 8%. However, a retiree may still select an RDR of 10% if his or her time-preference factor (i.e., impatience) is high. If, however, either of the two parameter estimates is inaccurate (e.g., if the return is lower than the estimated mean or the standard deviation is higher than estimated), then 8% may not be the optimal RDR. Pye suggests that 8% is probably not too far from the optimal value. Therefore, investors may still prefer to stick with 8% because they will be adequately compensated by the opportunity to avoid severe retrenchment in early retirement.

Pye (2012) stresses the importance of the subjective time preferencing/discount rate. He notes that a key objective of retirees "is to avoid low withdrawals at any time over their retirement. But retirees are likely to be more averse to low withdrawals early in retirement than later on. . . . If retirees are less averse to low withdrawals later in retirement this difference should be reflected in the utility function. To do so later withdrawals can be multiplied by an equivalence factor to make their effect on utility comparable to that of earlier withdrawals" (p. 271). This means that the retirement income goal is to maximize time-adjusted utility. For a simple utility function, each future time-adjusted withdrawal generates utility equal to that of the initial withdrawal divided by the time equivalence factor for the applicable future year. Retirees wishing to spend more in the early years of retirement will have a larger subjective time-preference rate. When the preferencing rate is equal to zero, the discounting is simply (1 + Risk-free rate). This discount rate is characteristic of a retiree who prefers a constant standard of living. Often, however, retirees "prefer some downward slope in their withdrawals" (p. 284).

Pye's (2012) modeling is based on a sophisticated treatment of input variables. He develops a two-state model based on market valuation measures (e.g., price-to-earnings ratio and dividend yield), and when the metrics suggest an abnormal valuation level, expected return is adjusted accordingly. However, Pye does not fall into the trap of market timing. Although it may be tempting to change the stock/bond weighting because of changes in relative valuation, doing so is often counterproductive: "This is not surprising as changes in valuation account for only a very small portion of changes in realized investment return" (p. 205). The model treats inflation as a stochastic variable and accounts for investment fees and, where appropriate, tax liabilities.

In contrast to Pye (2012), Collins et al. (2015b) present a retirement income risk model that accommodates customized patterns of retirement spending, including constant real consumption, front-loaded consumption, and back-loaded consumption. Assume, for example, that a retired investor's wealth is greater than the present value of periodic minimum threshold needs as determined by reference to an SPIA benchmark (i.e., the free boundary). Collins et al. modify a Fisher utility-based model by concurrently incorporating a state-preference utility function. In this configuration, optimal spending is a combination of

- a minimum floor income requiring a fixed constant-dollar distribution and

- a floating distribution component based on investor time-preference rates (e.g., the rate of consumption declines as age advances) and on spending constraints conforming to investor risk aversion to outliving financial assets, as well as investor preferences for gifting and bequests.

The free boundary conditions allow the investment adviser to recommend asset management elections based on an intelligent assessment of investment surplus in the face of dynamic consumption and terminal wealth preferences.

Conclusion

The trend in recent academic literature is away from building models that assume CRRA utility, normal distribution of asset returns, time-invariant volatility and correlation parameters, constant inflation, and fixed withdrawal formulas. Indeed, it is somewhat surprising that the practitioner-oriented literature continues to produce a multitude of articles seeking optimal spending and asset management strategies derived from portfolio models embracing such assumptions.

Advances in retirement income risk modeling are striking in terms of both the complexity of the models and the scope of insights engendered. However, many of the case studies offered in the literature do not comport comfortably with likely spending patterns faced in retirement. Retired investors rarely spend according to constraints established either by shortfall probability estimates or according to autopilot formulas like the 4% adjusted-for-inflation rule. Furthermore, the utility-based analysis underpinning many life-cycle models generates optimal consumption rules based on the form of a possibly linear utility function rather than on the practical choices and exigencies that the investor encounters. Financial planning recommendations flowing from such risk models appear to be highly sophisticated, but investors should be mindful that such recommendations often arise in highly artificial contexts.

For example, consider a spending pattern that an investor on the threshold of retirement might wish to test in terms a portfolio's ability to fund it adequately:

1. During each month of retirement, withdraw 1/12 of 1% of the average value of the portfolio calculated over the previous 36 months.

2. For the first 63 months (e.g., the time remaining on a mortgage obligation), distribute an additional $8,000 per month adjusted for inflation.

3. In months 64–180, reduce the additional distribution to $6,000 per month adjusted for inflation.

4. Thereafter, distribute a constant-dollar $4,000 per month decreasing at a 2% per year rate.

This pattern exhibits a consumption tilt toward the early stages of retirement. It combines a high degree of budgetary control with flexibility to reap the rewards of potential future portfolio increases. The distribution suggests that the investor is willing to decrease later-life consumption if he survives longer than 15 years. The late-in-life strategy might assume that the targeted percentage reduction in fixed-amount portfolio distributions may, to some extent, be offset by consumer price index (CPI) increases in the investor's

Social Security benefits and, if investment results are satisfactory, by the monthly 1/12 of 1% variable withdrawal element of the strategy.

The investor may value additional customization of the spending policy to test the economic consequences of making lifetime charitable or intrafamily gifts. As the investor decides how to implement retirement—when to retire, whether to work part-time, how to adjust spending, and so forth—there can be little doubt that attention is directed more toward finding out whether the portfolio can sustain the preferred cash flow pattern than toward, say, the historical success rate of the 4% withdrawal rate rule. Optimal retirement planning puts the investor in a position to reveal utility by selecting among various retirement spending patterns and terminal wealth outcomes. This process differs from budgets imposed by predetermined rules.

Even the sample spending pattern, however, is too neat. The retired investor faces a possibility of incurring unexpected financial emergencies that will force liquidation of financial assets. If dental expenses, home repairs, or other nondiscretionary outlays suddenly require unanticipated portfolio withdrawals, the expenses must be paid irrespective of whether they are accounted for in the annual budgeted withdrawal amount. If initial resources are modest, the investor often wrestles with the trade-off between the ability to sustain an aspirational standard of living and the possibility of future financial hardship. It is useful, as this literature survey makes patently clear, to distinguish between an aspirational standard of living and a threshold, or minimally acceptable standard of living. Although retirees seek to preserve the aspirational standard of living for as long as possible, they are constrained by the feasibility condition. That is, it is imprudent to engage in a level of current spending that creates a high probability of failing to meet threshold future living costs. If we cannot say that a commercial annuity constitutes the optimal retirement income path, we can infer that the prudent investor checks the portfolio's financial health against an annuity-based benchmark. The next section explores the nature and scope of such a benchmark in greater detail.

Part Three: A Survey of Academic Literature on Annuities

Estimating Annuity Costs and Loads and Utility

Previous sections of the literature review discuss (1) the merits of using a single premium immediate annuity as a monitoring and performance benchmark and (2) the merits of electing to annuitize some or all of financial wealth to guarantee lifetime periodic income payments. The latter asset management election is often evaluated in a life-cycle model that seeks to gauge the utility value of an actuarially fair annuity. Actuarially fair annuities are, however, unavailable to investors. The prudence of exercising an option to annuitize depends, of course, on a variety of factors, including contract costs. The cost of an actuarial solution determines the capital sacrifice required to transfer longevity risk from the investor to the insurance industry. That is, it quantifies the amount of wealth that must leave the financial asset portion of the retirement portfolio and enter the insurance contract portion in order to secure a target amount of periodic lifetime income.

There is a large body of research on the topic of annuity costs and benefits. Unless otherwise stated, this literature review focuses on SPIAs promising either fixed or inflation-adjusted payouts. The review begins in 1998, when Milevsky used a value per premium dollar (VPD) method to estimate an annuity's load. An actuarially fair annuity has a VPD equal to 1; a commercial annuity, if priced to be profitable for the issuer, has a VPD less than 1. The calculation formula is a two-step process. Step one sums, over a maximum possible lifetime (through age 115), the values of a fraction, where the numerator is a $1.00 periodic annuity payment adjusted for the probability that the annuitant is alive to receive it and the denominator is the applicable time-value-of-money discount rate. Step two evaluates the ratio of the sum of the discounted, probability-adjusted $1.00 payments (step one) to the current market price of an annuity contract. Milevsky estimates that the average annuity load for Canadian annuities during 1984–1996 is approximately 12% when discounting at the corporate bond rate. In much of the literature, VPD is also called "money's worth."

Mitchell et al. (1999) outline three methods to determine annuity costs and value:

1. The first method, which they term the expected present discounted value (EPDV) of an annuity, is the step one calculation of the VPD—the sum

of periodic mortality-adjusted payments discounted by an appropriate term structure of interest rates. The authors' estimate implies annuity costs of between 7% and 16%.

2. The second method calculates an annuity's internal rate of return. The IRR formula subtracts the commercial annuity price from the actuarially fair EPDV and solves for the EPDV discount rate that brings the cost difference to zero. The investor can determine the relative attractiveness of annuitizing some or all of current wealth by comparing the annuity IRR with that of other investments.

3. The third method of estimating annuity cost and value compares the expected utility gained by annuitization with the expected utility provided by other investment options. In this case, the authors calculate the percentage of wealth that must be annuitized in order to produce utility equal to the consumption that would take place absent annuitization. Specifically, the utility of financing consumption through risky investment is equivalent to a wealth reduction of between 30% and 38% when compared with financing consumption through an actuarially fair annuity for an age 65 investor exhibiting constant relative risk aversion.

Thus, assuming no preexisting annuity income, a CRRA investor could, in the authors' opinion, increase utility by annuitizing wealth even when facing loads as high as 30%.

James and Vittas (1999) define an annuity's money's worth ratio (MWR) as the present value of the expected stream of benefits divided by its initial cost, or in terms of the previous cost measures: EPDV/Market price of a commercial annuity. James and Vittas find that the MWR in many countries approaches 1 when discounted at the risk-free rate. Inflation-adjusted annuities, however, have ratio values 7%–9% lower than comparable nominal-payout annuities.

The comparatively high MWR ratio values found by James and Vittas (1999) are, in large part, a byproduct of their choice of discount rate. Future studies often use multiple discount rates—Treasuries, corporate bonds, mortgage-backed securities, and so forth. The MWR is highly sensitive to the discount rate choice, and therefore, care must be taken to understand how an economist or actuary calculates MWR. For example, the choice of the discount rate can reflect either the predominant components of insurance company investment portfolios (discounting from the seller's perspective) or reflect the rates of return available to annuity buyers (discounting from the buyer's perspective). Charupat, Kamstra, and Milevsky (2012) note that "the 10-year swap rates are the best match to the average duration of the annuities we look at" (p. 7). In calculating the MWR, Zwecher (2010) argues that annuity payments should be discounted at the cost of debt financing for the issuing carrier: "Insurance contracts for retirees are little more than corporate debt with a mortality pooling component; the correct rate to discount payments that an insurance contract will pay would be at the rate that the insurance company would pay to issue debt at that maturity" (p. 56).

Several research papers reconsider the assumptions underlying calculation of the MWR numerator. Selection of mortality data (e.g., general population mortality versus annuitant subpopulation mortality) significantly changes MWR values. Mitchell (2001) emphasizes this point: "Mortality processes may be heterogeneous across subgroups of the population" (p. 10). She develops the concept of annuity equivalent wealth (AEW), which first appears in Mitchell et al. (1999). Mitchell (2001) defines AEW as "the amount of wealth that a consumer would need *if he did not have access to an annuity market,* in order to achieve the same lifetime expected utility level that he could achieve by using that wealth to purchase a nominal annuity" (p. 7). An annuity contract guarantees a specified consumption level; a risky asset portfolio may or may not provide funds sufficient to meet future consumption needs. The AEW of an annuity for a highly risk-averse investor may be significantly positive despite the fact that the MWR is less than 1. Mitchell considers AEW under various inflation processes for consumers with no preexisting annuity benefits as well as for consumers who have previously annuitized half of their wealth (e.g., by claiming Social Security benefits). The inflation process confronting the investor has a significant impact on AEW, especially if the annuity payments are fixed in nominal terms. As a general rule, however, Mitchell finds, depending on the investor's coefficient of risk aversion under a CRRA model, that financial wealth earmarked for production of income must be adjusted upward by amounts ranging from 30% to more than 200% to provide utility values equal to annuitization. Risk-averse CRRA investors consider longevity insurance to be a valuable benefit.

The concept of AEW is further developed in Brown et al. (2001). The authors are primarily interested in determining the extent to which AEW can "overcome" an EPDV value of less than 1. Despite the fact that stocks offer a higher expected payout, they expose investors to market volatility and cannot guarantee a fixed real return. An alternative, under the authors' model, is a constant-dollar annuity. The AEW values for such a hypothetical, fair-valued annuity range from 1.502 to 2.004 for the coefficient of relative risk aversion ranging from 1 through 10. The model assumes an investor with no preexisting annuity income.

Although some commercial annuity contracts provide a constant-dollar income stream, such an income stream may not be optimal. When an investor

　　　　75

fails to exhibit a CRRA utility function or when the investor's personal (i.e., subjective) discount rate is high because consumption early in retirement is more highly valued than consumption toward the end of life (i.e., impatience), an annuity income may not prove attractive. Modeling flexibility becomes increasingly important in future research studies as retirement risk models begin to incorporate different assumptions regarding the structure of the utility function, the nature of the return-generating process, and the number of exogenous independent variables. Brown et al. (2001) review the annuity market in the United Kingdom and estimate that the EPDV of a nominal UK annuity is approximately 90% of the premium.

A further extension of the concept of AEW appears in Brown (2001), who employs dynamic programming to construct an AEW measure consistent with CRRA utility. Brown's model suggests that wealthier individuals are less likely to annuitize. Among the possible explanations are that wealthy investors

- are less likely to exhaust financial resources,

- have more preexisting annuity wealth,

- are more likely to try to earn high investment returns, or

- are more likely to have a bequest motive.

Brown, Mitchell, and Poterba (2002) find that the EPDV of a US annuity is between 80 and 90 cents per dollar of purchase price for members of the general population but between 90 and 100 cents per dollar for members of the annuitant-mortality table population—that is, for annuity buyers. Finally, Browne, Milevsky, and Salisbury (2003) argue that an actuarially fair annuity has less utility than it seems because of the high value placed by investors on liquidity, or access to their own money; thus, there is a large additional return required by these investors for holding an illiquid contract, such as a life annuity.

Milevsky (2006) introduces an annuity return measure called "implied longevity yield" (ILY). He notes that, assuming constant annuity pricing factors, the cost of providing a dollar of lifetime income at older ages is less than the cost at younger ages. The ILY is the investment return needed to withdraw an annuity cash flow measured at age x so that the investor has a sufficient portfolio value to purchase, at an older age y, an equal or greater lifetime annuity cash flow.

Of course, the risk of the strategy is either (1) that a lower-than-anticipated investment return fails to produce sufficient wealth to purchase an equivalent income stream or (2) that the future annuity cost increases because of changes in market interest rates or longevity expectations. Any self-annuitization plan must produce an earnings rate at least λ above the insurer's annuity pricing rate in order to make the self-annuitization plan reasonable. The investor must beat the insurer's pricing benchmark—cost of capital, bond portfolio return, and so forth—plus the annuity's mortality credits (λ). Solving for the ILY provides insight into the feasibility of a successful deferral: How likely is it that the investor can earn the ILY or better at a level of risk that is comfortable?

Although Milevsky (2006) adopts an option valuation approach to investment decision making, the concept of ILY captures some of the surveillance and monitoring issues faced by retired investors. Milevsky's discussion complements Li's (2008) analysis of the distribution of future annuity costs. Investors may face a critical asset management decision: As the value of the portfolio falls toward the free boundary, should they continue to own a risky-asset portfolio? Quantifying the yield required to sustain a self-annuitization investment strategy is a useful first step in prudent decision making.

Recent academic research into the value of annuitization usually employs a utility-based framework. Zahm and Ameriks (2012) is a noteworthy exception. They define IRR as "the rate the annuity payments are discounted to equate them to the annuity purchase price" (p. 2). It is difficult, in the authors' opinion, for consumers to know the cost of an annuity contract: "Purchasers simply see an all-in annuity quote as a single 'net yield' offering and must assess the attractiveness of the annuity arrangement on that all-in basis" (p. 5). An annuity load consists of four elements: (1) conservative pricing reflecting adverse selection risk to the insurer, (2) cost of maintaining a reserve against the risk that the annuitant population may realize greater-than-expected mortality improvements, (3) administrative costs, and (4) profit. The authors note that "costs arising from adverse selection in the insurance market and from administering the annuities are substantial" (p. 9). The IRR evaluation metric helps consumers determine whether annuitization is an attractive retirement income strategy. Given annuity contract pricing in year 2012, the authors calculate IRR for both nominal, shown in **Table 1**, and inflation-adjusted, shown in **Table 2**, contracts issued at various ages. The IRRs are based on the median life expectancy and

Table 1. Treasury Rate vs. IRR for Male, Female, and Joint Lives

Age	Treasury Rate	Male IRR	Female IRR	Joint IRR
65	3.02	3.27	3.27	3.18
70	3.02	2.37	2.69	2.74
75	2.28	0.52	1.81	2.04
80	2.28	−4.03	−0.55	0.45

Note: The 10-year securities are used for the 75- and 85-year-old purchaser; the 20-year security is used for the 65- and 70-year-old.

Table 2. Treasury Rate vs. Inflation-Adjusted IRR for Male, Female, and Joint Lives

Age	Treasury Rate	Male IRR	Female IRR	Joint IRR
65	0.74	−0.05	−0.08	−0.07
70	0.74	−0.95	−0.63	−0.38
75	0.19	−2.66	−1.36	−0.88
80	0.19	−7.75	−3.95	−2.54

Note: The 10-year securities are used for the 75- and 85-year-old purchaser; the 20-year security is used for the 65- and 70-year-old.

are based on 10- or 20-year US Treasuries or, for CPI-linked payouts, on 10- or 20-year TIPS.

These results suggest that few "general population" investors expecting to live for an average amount of time should purchase an annuity, given the pricing at the time of the study. However, Zahm and Ameriks (2012) also calculate IRRs for the top quartile of the population—the individuals who end up living longer than 75% of the population and, therefore, realize a better payoff. The authors conclude: "The internal rates of return for this group are all above current yields available on investments with comparable investment risk over similar horizons" (p. 7). Thus, those expecting to be in the top quartile of longevity might rationally wish to purchase annuities.

Brown (2011), revisiting and updating earlier research, concludes that annuities are not attractively priced for the general population: "First, insurance companies selling annuities need to cover administrative and marketing expenses and earn a competitive accounting profit. Second, to the extent that individuals who choose to annuitize have longer life expectancies than the general population, insurance companies need to adjust their prices to reflect this fact" (p. 61). The author estimates that "administrative costs account for a 3% to 5% reduction in annuity payouts. . . . Adverse selection is responsible for an 8% to 12% reduction in annuity payouts" (p. 62). He identifies a list of factors that may serve to reduce the value of a nominal annuity. For example, the welfare gains from annuitization are not as great for a married couple as they are for individual annuitants. Additionally, nominal annuities are particularly vulnerable to persistent inflation. Brown calculates that the purchase of a nominal joint and 50% survivor annuity in a 3.2% annual inflation environment by a household with a 65-year-old man and 62-year-old woman who have 50% of wealth preannuitized generates an AEW of 0.88: "That is, the couple faces a 12% load factor on their annuity purchase" (p. 66).

Any utility-based measure of annuitization is, of course, model dependent. The classic life-cycle models of consumption smoothing—savings during working years and decumulation of financial assets during retirement—generally solve for utility optimization. As we cautioned earlier, readers of academic papers should be aware of the implications of the choice of utility function for the retirement income model. Gong and Webb (2010) note that their model's outputs on the annuity equivalent value of both inflation-adjusted and nominal annuities are highly sensitive to the use of CRRA utility: "The above calculations are contingent on a utility function that does not appear to be very predictive of current behavior. . . . Care needs to be taken when estimating the distribution of welfare gains with an expected utility framework that has substantive predictions so at odds with observed behavior" (p. 220).[55]

As noted, models structured to provide closed-form solutions are possible only in the face of a host of simplifying assumptions, including market completeness—that is, financial products and strategies span all risks; the nature of the equity risk premium, often considered to be static and independent of other state variables, such as interest rates; and not surprisingly, the form of the utility function. The majority of models restrict the investment portfolio to two asset classes (risky equity plus a risk-free bond) in which portfolio returns evolve according to a Brownian motion process.

Menoncin and Scaillet (2003) provide a good example of building a closed-form model for maximizing utility. In this case, the authors solve the well-known Hamilton–Jacobi–Bellman equation[56] for optimal utility and conclude that investors should, with the exception of a hedging component, generally stay the course with respect to an asset allocation based on the Merton optimum.[57] However, they acknowledge that their conclusions depend on a model that incorporates strong assumptions. This is especially the case for the CRRA assumption: "It is well known that the value function usually inherits its functional form from the utility function" (p. 19). Indeed, the optimal allocation to the risky asset, although independent of both real

---

[55]Empirical evidence indicates that the subgroup of wealthy retirees who are most likely to seek investment advice exhibit decreasing relative risk aversion (DRRA). See, for example, Carroll (2000).

[56]A discussion of the Hamilton–Jacobi–Bellman value equation together with its use in dynamic optimization is found in Chapter 14 of Charupat, Huang, and Milevsky (2012).

[57]The Merton optimum is derived by multiplying the reciprocal of an investor's coefficient of risk aversion by a fraction, the numerator of which is the risk premium, or expected return on the risky asset portfolio minus the risk-free rate, and the denominator of which is the estimated portfolio variance. The structural form of the fraction is similar to the Sharpe ratio. In the case of log utility, the portfolio exhibiting the highest value for the Merton optimum is frequently termed the "growth optimal portfolio."

wealth and price level, is heavily dependent "on the choice of both the utility function and the functional form chosen for the drift and diffusion terms of assets, price level, and inflation" (p. 22).

Decomposition of Annuity Costs

Several studies provide a more direct cost estimate by decomposing the annuity contract into its underlying sales, administrative, investment, and actuarial elements. For example, Sell, Cooperstein, and Jessen (2004) provide the following estimates based on a survey of insurance carriers offering single premium immediate annuities:

- "On average, for the longer payout options, the compensation is about 3% to 5%. For the shorter payout options, it is 1.5% to 3%. . . . The lowest average was in the wirehouse channel at 3.3%, and the highest was in the independent producer channel at 4.3%" (p. 4).

- "Expenses are all over the place. . . . On average, this is about 80 bps on the premium side and $235 per contract. Similarly, on the maintenance-expense side, we typically see a per-policy and basis points of assets. Averages were $55 per contract there and 12 bps" (p. 4).

- "For common target surplus assumptions, by far the majority of them hold a percent of statutory reserves that is about 4.3%. Some incorporate a premium component, and that averages 3.8% of statutory reserves, plus 4.84% of premium. On average, these levels represent about 250% of NAIC [National Association of Insurance Commissioners] risk-based capital (RBC)" (p. 5).

- "For pricing targets, we did not ask them what actual profitability they were realizing, but by far again, the majority use statutory internal rate of return (IRR) as the pricing measure. It averages about 12%. The second most common measure is GAAP return on equity (ROE), and it has similar ranges and averages as the statutory IRR" (p. 5).

- "We asked our survey participants to report what their average asset mix was for their immediate annuities, and about 70% of the assets were in investment-grade corporate and commercial mortgages" (p. 5).

- "Similar to expenses, the required interest spreads are all over the place. Because you have so many different product designs, some contracts do not have any loads; some have policy fees, annual loads, and upfront percent of premium loads, so it is difficult to generalize spreads. They ranged in our survey from 50 bps to 320 bps. . . . On average, we saw a spread of about 118 bps for a five-year period certain and 89 bps for a single life option" (p. 5).

Weinsier (2005) provides further insights:

- "In terms of profit measures, you have the traditional IRR measure. . . . Profit margin is popular obviously, return on assets, GAAP ROE. . . . Most folks are still shooting for that 12% IRR" (p. 10).

- "What about the impact of interest rates, obviously a key moving part to your fixed annuities? I think we all know that low rates cause spread compression. With a low sustained rate, your higher earning assets end by going over (i.e., maturing), you have to invest them low, that brings your portfolio yield down, and you are going to realize spread compression. On the other hand, a rapid rise in rates is no picnic either. If we see all of a sudden a very rapid rise, then you would likely get some surrender mediation occurring [i.e., disintermediation by policyholders seeking the benefits of a higher return]" (p. 12).

Dellinger (2011) also makes several observations on annuity pricing:

- "Fixed immediate annuities contain a 'spread' between the earned rate on underlying assets (e.g., bonds and other fixed-income securities in the insurer's general account portfolio segment backing fixed immediate annuity obligations) and the credited rate on the liability (e.g., fixed immediate annuity reserve). This spread, in essence parallels its expense charge counterpart on registered products" (p. 21).

- "The load, when it exists, is typically a 'percentage of premium' charge used to cover acquisition expenses such as wholesaler compensation, financial adviser sales compensation, policy issuance, record set-up and other policy acquisition expenses as well as state premium tax, if applicable" (p. 27).[58]

When compared with the benefits generated by an actuarially fair annuity, a variety of costs decrement the value received by investors buying an annuity contract in the marketplace.

Finally, Nielson (2012) observes that most annuities are sold by firms managing large blocks of life insurance. Some of these companies may be able to offer better-than-expected annuity returns because "the sale of an annuity

---

[58]Dellinger (2011) also presents a case for early annuitization under specific economic circumstances: "Sometimes people believe they should wait to purchase an income annuity until a later date because the mortality credits are higher at higher ages" (p. 8). Although this assertion is correct, Dellinger asserts that the "purchase of an income annuity at a later date negates income attributable to mortality credits the purchaser could have enjoyed had he or she purchased the income annuity at an earlier date" (p. 8). In other words, the election to annuitize trades the incremental benefits of marginally higher current income for the possibility of receiving a much greater income entitlement at a more advanced age. In Dellinger's model, the need for greater immediate income is the primary driver in the decision-making process. If there is no need for extra current income, it makes sense to postpone annuitization.

reduces the overall risk faced by the firm and produces a corresponding reduction in the needed (risk-adjusted) rate of return" (p. 8).

Are Annuities Risk Free?

Annuities are not risk-free assets because they depend on the issuing carrier's financial ability to fulfill the terms of the contract. Excellent treatments of this issue are found in Babbel and Merrill (2007), Borzi and Patterson (2008), Munnell (2008), and Pharies (2010).

Crawford et al. (2008) note that annuities are not financial instruments with payoffs orthogonal to the capital markets. They are backed by bond portfolios and are guaranteed by corporations operating within the markets. Bond default risk increases the risk that an annuity will fail. They caution:

- "Currently . . . insurers tend to back their annuity liabilities with a significant amount of corporate debt. These investments have inherent risk of default, which would leave the insurer with less assets than expected to provide for the annuity payments in situations where economic growth was slowed below expected levels, or the economy was in recession" (p. 25).

- "Adverse mortality experience, whether higher or lower than expected, has implications for reserving and for capital requirements if the ability of the life industry to raise capital becomes impaired based on the market's perception of the variability of life company debt" (p. 23).

- "The lives that purchase annuities can be very different to those who purchase life insurance. Thus, companies that use natural hedging to manage longevity risk are, therefore, exposed to basis risk" (p. 37).

These observations have important implications both for financial advisers and for builders of retirement income risk models. Incorporating the risk of carrier insolvency into risk models can significantly reduce the attractiveness of annuities measured in either utility or dollar wealth space. A good example of incorporating the risk of counterparty default is found in Pang (2002).

Milevsky (2013) notes:

- "More than 165,000 policyholders had purchased high-yield annuities from Baldwin-United, and the money was frozen for more than three years while regulators and the courts picked up the piece. Another saga that has been ongoing for 20 years. . . is Executive Life Insurance Company of New York" (p. 25).

- "NOLHGA (National Organization of Life & Health Insurance Guaranty Associations) has been active recently in the following instances: When

Golden State Mutual Life Insurance was shut down by regulators in California in September 2009; when Shenandoah Life entered receivership in Virginia in February 2009; when Standard Life Insurance Company of Indiana was taken over by Indiana regulators in December 2008; and when London Pacific Life & Annuity Company was liquidated in July 2004" (p. 26).

- "The concept of diversification applies not only to stocks and bonds, but also to insurance policies, including life annuities" (p. 27).

Financial advisers should consider the consequences of a failure to diversify the annuity portfolio in light of both potential carrier insolvencies and limitations in state insurance guarantee funds.[59]

Interest Rates, Equity Market Performance, and the Annuity Purchase Decision

Some studies consider the impact of interest rate changes on the timing of an annuity purchase decision. For example, Poterba (2001) questions the wisdom of purchasing an annuity in a low interest rate environment. He cautions that annuitizing all wealth at once is a type of annuity market timing. Annuity yields are a function of interest rates, and given the substantial variation in rates over time, it may be unwise to trade all financial wealth for an annuity income stream based on the interest rate prevailing at any single moment—especially, of course, when interest rates are low because, all else being equal, annuity costs decrease as interest rates rise. Orszag (2002b) provides a counterpoint by noting that, although annuities are expensive in a low interest rate environment, the ratio of annuity income to bond income may be attractive because of the mortality credit. The lower the interest rate, the greater the relative impact of the credit.[60]

An investor may wish to maintain exposure to a portfolio of risky assets in order to exploit the opportunity to achieve an increase in wealth sufficient to lock in a future income in excess of that which an annuity offers today. Ameriks and Ren (2008) stake out this position: "Given ongoing variability in both prices and spending needs, many people might do better by continuing to share in the risks and returns of a well-chosen and diversified set of investments as a resource for their cash flow. Compared with fixed payments, certain assets may be more volatile but also may provide a far better means to hedge spending risks such as inflation over long periods" (p. 7).

However, by following such a strategy, the investor incurs two risks: (1) the investment returns may be poorer than expected or (2) the cost of the annuity

---

[59]*Best's Key Rating Guide* lists guaranty fund provisions for each state.
[60]The costs of nonqualified annuities over the period July 1992–July 2012 is detailed in Brien and Panis (2011).

83

might outpace the realized returns on the investment portfolio. In either case, instead of being rewarded for taking risk, the investor may discover that she must suffer a diminished future standard of living. Milevsky and Young (2002) discuss these risks in detail. A decision to delay annuitization in the hopes of improving the future budget constraint by out-earning the annuity is equivalent to taking a chance on interest rate movements and equity market performance. Milevsky and Young's observations are echoed by Abels (2005). He notes: "People are not as inclined to lock in those low-interest rates. They do not want to lock in the payouts that result from calculating them in low-interest rates for the rest of their life" (p. 11).

A broad cross section of commentators caution investors not to rush into annuity solutions during the current period of historically low interest rates. Horneff et al. (2008) voice the opinion: "Even if interest rates are stochastic, retirees will do well to wait until age 80 in the current low-interest rate environment" (p. 397). They explore the interrelationships among interest rates, investor risk aversion, and the demand to annuitize. As a general rule, the higher the interest rate, the sooner the retiree elects to annuitize. The authors write:

> However, a more risk-loving retiree will also demand a higher short rate than her risk-averse counterpart. The switching frontier itself is concave because the mortality credit increases over time and replaces cost advantages formerly generated by the related short rate. Interestingly, the advice about when to switch to annuities depends on the current level of the short rate, as it relates to the level of mean reversion. The retiree would likely want to wait until age 80 to annuitize if the short rate is below the long-term mean and mean reversion is anticipated. . . . The lower the risk aversion, the higher the short rate must be to induce the retiree to annuitize her assets. (p. 405)

The elegance and complexity of these observations demonstrate the importance of retirement income monitoring and surveillance programs designed to help investors make intelligent asset management decisions. Financial advisers must ask themselves about the wisdom of recommending annuitization in a historically low interest rate environment given the mean-reversionary tendencies of short-term interest rates.

Previtero (2011) highlights the risk of annuitizing wealth at a specific moment in time. He calculates that annuitizing after the market drop of 2009 reduced retirement welfare by as much as 10%. Zahm and Ameriks (2012) illustrate how a change in interest rates can dramatically affect payout amounts offered to contract buyers. For example, for a 65-year-old male, the annuity payout amount decreased by 8.85% on the nominal benefit contract and 6.07% on the inflation-adjusted payout contract between 20 April 2011 and 27 October 2011, a period when Treasury rates declined sharply.

Finally, Warshawsky (2012) provides a broader historical view of the risk of trying to time annuity purchases:

> At the end of May 1984, a $100,000 premium bought a monthly payout of $1,134 for a couple. By the end of June 2003, however, as interest rates fell to secular lows, the same $100,000 bought only $503 in fixed monthly lifetime benefits. . . . By 30 December 2008, the fixed monthly lifetime payment on newly issued SPIAs had dropped to only $417 before recovering throughout 2009 to the $500 level. (p. 40)

Conclusion

The literature on longevity risk and portfolio sustainability is, to a great extent, a history of risk modeling. Throughout the 50 years covered in this literature survey, researchers have developed a set of decision-making tools to explore, under conditions of uncertainty, dynamic relationships among key variables. Often, there are twin goals of understanding the nature of these relationships and of suggesting salutary asset management strategies for retirement income portfolios.

One important—and still emerging—theme is that asset management requires credible monitoring and surveillance policies as complex portfolios, operating under conditions of stress, present critical choices to investors seeking to adapt to evolving personal and economic conditions. Modern commentary on this subject tends to view retirement income portfolios as bundles of asset management elections that may be intelligently assessed and implemented to either mitigate risk or capitalize on an investment opportunity. Indeed, to a certain extent, a retirement income portfolio can be viewed as a stream of cash flow targets plus a set of management options.

Early published research defined important issues and began a critical examination of important topics. Often, however, early models focused on only a few variables of interest and, given computational restrictions, used simple inputs, such as a stylized two-asset investment portfolio generating lognormal return distributions under a constant inflation process. Sometimes, decision making, in the form of spending rules, was set in stone at the beginning of the planning horizon. No matter how events unfolded in the future, the linear, closed-form solutions demanded by a risk model's underlying mathematics prohibited any contingent decision-making activity. Future investment decisions are fixed at the outset; circumstances may change, but the model's structure does not. Portfolio monitoring and surveillance, by definition, is of secondary importance in such a highly artificial context. The focus of normative models has been on providing asset allocation design and implementation advice capable of withstanding the stress of preset spending targets. In some cases, research efforts focused on the elusive task of discovering an "all-weather" investment and withdrawal policy. Other researchers recommend investing heavily in equity if the investor needs to provide ample money for a lifetime. These approaches are static or architectural approaches to investment policy, and they are often coupled with asset allocations that maintain a fixed and permanent vector of investment weights.

Some of the later research moves away from this paradigm toward a view that sees asset allocation as the economic contribution of investments thoughtfully arranged to capitalize on unfolding events. The legal profession expresses this concept of prudent asset management with the phrase "care, skill, and caution." The necessity of building in a portfolio review process elevates the significance of portfolio monitoring; that is, it creates the precondition for contingent decision making between investment and actuarial solution paths or among various financial management solution paths.

The nature of future uncertainty is itself uncertain and, depending on circumstances, will reveal dangers and opportunities unexpected at the moment of retirement. At first blush, it seems that risk-averse investors, valuing an early and complete resolution of uncertainty, may find that annuitization is the utility-maximizing option. However, the risk-averse investors may conclude that annuitization is an irreversible decision that both diminishes liquidity and restrains future consumption opportunities. Given such drawbacks, there is a value, *if economically feasible*, to delaying the option to implement the actuarial solution—at least to delay full implementation—until future events resolve the investor's uncertainty. The risk–reward trade-off in this context is the reduction of an investor's exposure to uncertainty versus the irrevocable sacrifice of investment capital and the potential returns thereon.

This brings the discussion to the feasibility topic. Although there are many books and articles on asset allocation strategies and withdrawal formulas for retirement income portfolios, there is only a scant amount of advice on how to monitor wealth to assess whether goals continue to remain attainable. If current portfolio value is less than retirement liabilities, the portfolio is technically insolvent. Investors can hope that things will work out satisfactorily, but they cannot expect them to do so. Investing encompasses monitoring. As private investors are asked to fill the void created by the decrease in guaranteed corporate-sponsored or public pension income, presenting a clear, unbiased, and credible assessment of the retirement portfolio's evolving financial health is an increasingly important aspect of managing longevity risk and retirement income planning.[61]

---

[61]The authors would like to thank Laurence Siegel, Mary-Kate Hines, and Abby Farson Pratt for their many helpful editorial suggestions.

Bibliography

Abbas, Ali E., and James E. Matheson. 2005. "Normative Target-Based Decision Making." *Managerial and Decision Economics*, vol. 26, no. 6 (September): 373–385.

Abels, Stephen J. 2005. "Payout and Income Annuities." *Society of Actuaries Record*, vol. 31, no. 1 (May): 1–26.

Albrecht, Peter, and Raimond Maurer. 2001. "Self-Annuitization, Ruin Risk in Retirement and Asset Allocation: The Annuity Benchmark." Working paper (www.actuaries.org/AFIR/Colloquia/Toronto/Albrecht_Maurer.pdf).

Ameriks, John, and Liqian Ren. 2008. "Generating Guaranteed Income: Understanding Income Annuities." Vanguard Investment Counseling & Research.

Ameriks, John, and Paul Yakoboski. 2003. "Reducing Retirement Income Risks: The Role of Annuitization." *Benefits Quarterly*, vol. 19, no. 4 (Fourth Quarter): 13–24.

Ameriks, John, Andres Caplin, Steven Laufer, and Stijn Van Nieuwerburgh. 2008. "Annuity Valuation, Long-Term Care, and Bequest Motives." In *Recalibrating Retirement Spending and Saving*. Edited by John Ameriks and Olivia S. Mitchell. London: Oxford University Press.

Amihud, Yakov, and Haim Mendelson. 1986. "Liquidity and Stock Returns." *Financial Analysts Journal*, vol. 42, no. 3 (May/June): 43–48.

Babbel, David F., and Craig B. Merrill. 2007. "Rational Decumulation." Wharton Financial Institutions Center Working Paper No. 06–14 (22 May): http://fic.wharton.upenn.edu/fic/papers/06/0614.pdf.

Bajtelsmit, Vickie, LeAndra Ottem Foster, and Anna Rappaport. 2013. "Strategies for Mitigating the Risk of Outliving Retirement Wealth." *Financial Services Review*, vol. 22, no. 4 (Winter): 311–329.

Bajtelsmit, Vickie, Anna Rappaport, and LeAndra Foster. 2013. "Measures of Retirement Benefit Adequacy: Which, Why, for Whom, and How Much?" Society of Actuaries' Pension Section and Pension Section Research Committee (January): www.soa.org/Files/Research/Projects/research-2013-measures-retirement.pdf.

Balls, Kim G. 2006. "Immediate Annuity Pricing in the Presence of Unobserved Heterogeneity." *North American Actuarial Journal*, vol. 10, no. 4 (December): 103–116.

Barro, Robert J. 2009. "Rare Disasters, Asset Prices, and Welfare Costs." *American Economic Review*, vol. 99, no. 1 (March): 243–264.

Bengen, William P. 1994. "Determining Withdrawal Rates Using Historical Data." *Journal of Financial Planning*, vol. 7, no. 4 (October): 171–180.

Bierwirth, Larry. 1994. "Investing for Retirement: Using the Past to Model the Future." *Journal of Financial Planning*, vol. 7, no. 1 (January): 14–24.

Blake, David, Andrew J.G. Cairns, and Kevin Dowd. 2003. "Pensionmetrics 2: Stochastic Pension Plan Design during the Distribution Phase." *Insurance, Mathematics & Economics*, vol. 33, no. 1 (August): 29–47.

Blanchett, David M. 2013. "Examining the Benefits of Immediate Fixed Annuities in Today's Low-Rate Climate." *Journal of Financial Planning*, vol. 26, no. 1 (January): 42–50.

———. 2014. "Estimating the True Cost of Retirement." Presented at the Living to 100 Symposium, Orlando, Florida (8–10 January): www.soa.org/library/monographs/life/living-to-100/2014/mono-li14-1a-blanchett.aspx.

Borzi, Phyllis C., and Martha Priddy Patterson. 2008. "Regulating Markets for Retirement Payouts: Solvency, Supervision, and Credibility." In *Recalibrating Retirement Spending and Savings*. Edited by John Ameriks and Olivia S. Mitchell. London: Oxford University Press.

Brien, Michael J., and Constantijn W.A. Panis. 2011. "Annuities in the Context of Defined Contribution Plans." US Department of Labor, Employee Benefits Security Administration (November): 1–18.

Brown, Jeffrey R. 2001. "Private Pensions, Mortality Risk, and the Decision to Annuitize." *Journal of Public Economics*, vol. 82, no. 1 (October): 29–62.

———. 2011. "Longevity-Insured Retirement Distributions: Basic Theories and Institutions." In *Retirement Income: Risks and Strategies*. Edited by Mark J. Warshawsky. Cambridge, MA: MIT Press.

Brown, Jeffrey R., Olivia S. Mitchell, and James M. Poterba. 2001. "The Role of Real Annuities and Indexed Bonds in an Individual Accounts Retirement Program." In *The Role of Annuity Markets in Financing Retirement*. Edited by Jeffrey R. Brown, Olivia S. Mitchell, James M. Poterba, and Mark J. Warshawsky. Cambridge, MA: MIT Press.

———. "Mortality Risk, Inflation Risk, and Annuity Products." In *Innovations in Retirement Financing*. Edited by Olivia S. Mitchell, Zvi

Bodie, P. Brett Hammond, and Stephen Zeldes. Philadelphia: University of Pennsylvania Press: 175–197.

Brown, Robert L., and Patricia L. Scahill. 2010. "Issues in the Issuance of Enhanced Annuities." McMaster University Series: Social and Economic Dimensions of an Aging Population, Research Paper No. 265 (May): 1–12.

Browne, Sid. 1999. "The Risk and Rewards of Minimizing Shortfall Probability." *Journal of Portfolio Management*, vol. 25, no. 4 (Summer): 76–85.

Browne, Sid, Moshe A. Milevsky, and T.S. Salisbury. 2003. "Asset Allocation and the Liquidity Premium for Illiquid Annuities." *Journal of Risk and Insurance*, vol. 70, no. 3 (September): 509–526.

Browning, Martin, and Thomas F. Crossley. 2001. "The Lifecycle Model of Consumption and Saving." *Journal of Economic Perspectives*, vol. 15, no. 3 (Summer): 3–22.

Carroll, Christopher D. 2000. "Portfolios of the Rich." NBER Working Paper No. 7826 (August).

Cassidy, Daniel P., Michael W. Peskin, Laurence B. Siegel, and Stephen Sexauer. 2013. "Be Kind to Your Retirement Decumulation Plan—Give It a Benchmark." *Journal of Retirement*, vol. 1, no. 1 (Summer): 81–90.

Charupat, Narat, Huaxiong Huang, and Moshe A. Milevsky. 2012. *Strategic Financial Planning Over the Lifecycle: A Conceptual Approach to Personal Risk Management.* New York: Cambridge University Press.

Charupat, Narat, Mark J. Kamstra, and Moshe A. Milevsky. 2012. "The Annuity Duration Puzzle." Working paper (14 March).

Chen, Peng, and Moshe A. Milevsky. 2003. "Merging Asset Allocation and Longevity Insurance: An Optimal Perspective on Payout Annuities." *Journal of Financial Planning*, vol. 16, no. 6 (June): 52–62.

Collins, Patrick J. 2015. "An Annotated Bibliography: Longevity Risk and Portfolio Sustainability (1965–2014)." San Francisco, CA: Schultz Collins, Inc. (http://schultzcollins.com/static/uploads/2015/07/Annotated-bibliography.pdf).

———. 2016. *Annuities and Retirement Income Planning.* Charlottesville, VA: CFA Institute Research Foundation.

Collins, Patrick J., and Huy D. Lam. 2011. "Asset Allocation, Human Capital, and the Demand to Hold Life Insurance in Retirement." *Financial Services Review*, vol. 20, no. 4 (Winter): 303–325.

Collins, Patrick J., Huy D. Lam, and Josh Stampfli. 2015a. "How Risky Is Your Retirement Income Risk Model?" Working paper (13 May): http://papers.ssrn.com/sol3/papers.cfm?abstract_id=2548651.

———. 2015b. "Monitoring and Managing a Retirement Income Portfolio." *Retirement Management Journal: Between the Issues.* Salem State University (December).

Collins, Patrick J., Sam L. Savage, and Josh Stampfli. 2000. "Financial Consequences of Distribution Elections from Total Return Trusts." *Real Property, Probate, and Trust Journal*, vol. 35, no. 2 (Summer): 243–304.

Collins, Patrick J., and Josh Stampfli. 2001. "Promises and Pitfalls of Total Return Trusts." *ACTEC Law Journal*, vol. 27, no. 3 (Winter): 205–219.

———. 2009. "Managing Private Wealth: Matching Investment Policy to Investor Risk Preferences." *Banking Law Journal*, vol. 126, no. 10 (November): 923–957.

Crawford, Thomas, Richard de Haan, and Chad Runchey. 2008. "Longevity Risk Quantification and Management: A Review of Relevant Literature." Society of Actuaries (November): www.soa.org/Research/Research-Projects/Life-Insurance/research-long-risk-quant.aspx.

Davidoff, Thomas, Jeffrey Brown, and Peter Diamond. 2003. "Annuities and Individual Welfare." Pensions Institute Discussion Paper PI-0307 (May).

Davis, James L. 2010. "Spending Rates, Asset Allocation, and Probability of Failure." Dimensional Research Paper (May).

Dellinger, Jeffrey K. 2011. "When to Commence Income Annuities." Society of Actuaries: www.soa.org/library/monographs/retirement-systems/retirement-security/mono-2011-mrs12-dellinger-paper.pdf.

DiCarlo, Donald P., and Steven M. Fast. 2008. "Prudence: What Are the Odds?" In ALI-ABA Course of Study, *Representing Estate and Trust Beneficiaries and Fiduciaries.* San Francisco: American Law Institute and American Bar Association.

Diecidue, Enrico, and Jeroen Van De Ven. 2008. "Aspiration Level, Probability of Success and Failure, and Expected Utility." *International Economic Review*, vol. 49, no. 2 (May): 683–700.

Dus, Ivica, Raimond Maurer, and Olivia S. Mitchell. 2005. "Betting on Death and Capital Markets in Retirement: A Shortfall Risk Analysis of Life

Annuities versus Phased Withdrawal Plans." *Financial Services Review*, vol. 14, no. 3 (Fall): 169–196.

Dybvig, Philip H. 1999. "Using Asset Allocation to Protect Spending." *Financial Analysts Journal*, vol. 55, no. 1 (January/February): 49–62.

Epstein, Larry G., and Stanley E. Zin. 1989. "Substitution, Risk Aversion, and the Temporal Behavior of Consumption and Asset Returns: A Theoretical Framework." *Econometrica*, vol. 57, no. 4 (July): 937–969.

Ezra, Don. 2009. "Who Should Buy a Lifetime Income Annuity? And When?" CFA Institute, Private Wealth Management Feature Article (February): www.cfapubs.org/doi/full/10.2469/pwmn.v2009.n1.10.

Finke, Michael, Wade D. Pfau, and Duncan Williams. 2012. "Spending Flexibility and Safe Withdrawal Rates." *Journal of Financial Planning*, vol. 25, no. 3 (March): 44–51.

Fishburn, Peter C. 1977. "Mean-Risk Analysis with Risk Associated with Below-Target Returns." *American Economic Review*, vol. 67, no. 2 (March): 116–126.

Fisher, Irving. 1930. *The Theory of Interest: As Determined by Impatience to Spend Income and Opportunity to Invest It*. New York: Macmillan.

Frank, Larry R., John B. Mitchell, and David M. Blanchett. 2011. "An Age-Based, Three Dimensional, Universal Distribution Model Incorporating Sequence and Longevity Risks." Presented at the Academy of Financial Services, Las Vegas (23 October): www.academyfinancial.org/wp-content/uploads/2013/10/A1-Frank-Mitchell-Blanchett.pdf.

Friedman, Avner. 2000. "Free Boundary Problems in Science and Technology." *Notices of the American Mathematical Society*, vol. 47, no. 8 (September): 854–861.

Fullmer, Richard K. 2007. "Modern Portfolio Decumulation: A New Strategy for Managing Retirement Income." *Journal of Financial Planning*, vol. 20, no. 8 (August): 40–51.

Gerrard, Russell, Steven Haberman, and Elena Vigna. 2004. "Optimal Investment Choices Post-Retirement in a Defined Contribution Pension Scheme." *Insurance, Mathematics & Economics*, vol. 35, no. 2 (October): 321–342.

———. 2006. "The Management of Decumulation Risks in a Defined Contribution Pension Plan." *North American Actuarial Journal*, vol. 10, no. 1 (January): 84–110.

Gerrard, Russell, Bjarne Hojgaard, and Elena Vigna. 2012. "Choosing the Optimal Annuitization Time Post-Retirement." *Quantitative Finance*, vol. 12, no. 7 (July): 1143–1159.

Gong, Guan, and Anthony Webb. 2010. "Evaluating the Advanced Life Deferred Annuity—An Annuity People Might Actually Buy." *Insurance, Mathematics & Economics*, vol. 46, no. 1 (February): 210–221.

Gupta, Aparna, and Zhisheng Li. 2007. "Integrating Optimal Annuity Planning with Consumption-Investment Selections in Retirement Planning." *Insurance, Mathematics & Economics*, vol. 41, no. 1 (July): 96–110.

Harlow, W.V., and Keith C. Brown. 2014. "Market Risk, Mortality Risk, and Sustainable Retirement Asset Allocation: A Downside Risk Perspective." Working paper (29 December): http://faculty.mccombs.utexas.edu/keith.brown/Research/retireallocate-wp.pdf.

Horneff, Wolfram J., Raimond H. Maurer, Olivia S. Mitchell, and Ivica Dus. 2008. "Following the Rules: Integrating Asset Allocation and Annuitization in Retirement Portfolios." *Insurance, Mathematics & Economics*, vol. 42, no. 1 (February): 396–408.

Horneff, Wolfram J., Raimond H. Maurer, and Michael Z. Stamos. 2006. "Life-Cycle Asset Allocation with Annuity Markets: Is Longevity Insurance a Good Deal?" Michigan Retirement Research Center Research Paper No. 2006-146 (December).

Huang, Huaxiong, and Moshe A. Milevsky. 2008. "Portfolio Choice and Mortality-Contingent Claims: The General HARA Case." *Journal of Banking & Finance*, vol. 32, no. 11 (November): 2444–2452.

Hughen, J. Christopher, Francis E. Laatsch, and Daniel P. Klein. 2002. "Withdrawal Patterns and Rebalancing Costs for Taxable Portfolios." *Financial Services Review*, vol. 11, no. 4 (Winter): 341–366.

Hurst, Erik. 2008. "Understanding Consumption in Retirement: Recent Developments." In *Recalibrating Retirement Spending and Saving*. Edited by John Ameriks and Olivia S. Mitchell. Oxford, UK: Oxford University Press.

James, Estelle, and Dimitri Vittas. 1999. "Annuity Markets in Comparative Perspective. Do Consumers Get Their Money's Worth?" World Bank, Policy Research Working Papers (November): http://elibrary.worldbank.org/doi/abs/10.1596/1813-9450-2493.

Jones, Bruce L. 2000. "Analysis of Financial Needs in Retirement: A Multistate Approach." In *Retirement Needs Framework*. Society of Actuaries Monograph M-RS00-1 (January): 81–86.

Kapur, Sandeep, and J. Michael Orszag. 2002. "Portfolio Choice and Retirement Income Solutions." Watson Wyatt Technical Report 2002-RU05 (April).

Kingston, Geoffrey, and Susan Thorp. 2005. "Annuitization and Asset Allocation with HARA Utility." *Journal of Pension Economics and Finance*, vol. 4, no. 3 (November): 225–248.

Kitces, Michael. 2012. "Is the Retirement Plan with the Lowest 'Risk of Failure' Really the Best Choice?" Blog post (1 March): www.kitces.com/blog/ Is-The-Retirement-Plan-With-The-Lowest-Risk-of-Failure-Really-The-Best-Choice.

Korn, R., and M. Krekel. 2002. "Optimal Portfolios with Fixed Consumption or Income Streams." Working paper, Frauhofer-Institut fur Techno-und Wirtschaftsmathematic.

Levy, Haim, and Moshe Levy. 2009. "The Safety First Expected Utility Model: Experimental Evidence and Economic Implications." *Journal of Banking & Finance*, vol. 33, no. 8 (August): 1494–1506.

Li, Feng. 2008. "Ruin Problem in Retirement under Stochastic Return Rate and Mortality Rate and its Applications." Unpublished master's thesis, Simon Fraser University (Spring).

MacDonald, Bonnie-Jeanne, Bruce Jones, Richard J. Morrison, Robert L. Brown, and Mary Hardy. 2013. "Research and Reality—A Literature Review on Drawing Down Retirement Financial Savings." Society of Actuaries, Pension Section (23 June): www.soa.org/files/research/projects/research-literature-review-report.pdf.

Maurer, Raimond, Peter Albrecht, and Ulla Ruckpaul. 2001. "Shortfall-Risks of Stocks in the Long Run." *Financial Markets and Portfolio Management*, vol. 15, no. 4 (December): 481–499.

McGoun, Elton G. 1995. "The History of Risk Measurement." *Critical Perspectives on Accounting*, vol. 6, no. 6 (December): 511–532.

Menoncin, Francesco, and Olivier Scaillet. 2003. "Mortality Risk and Real Optimal Asset Allocation for Pension Funds." Working paper (www.ifid.ca/ conference_material/menoncin_paper.pdf).

Milevsky, Moshe A. 1998. "Optimal Asset Allocation Towards the End of the Live Cycle: To Annuitize or Not to Annuitize." *Journal of Risk and Insurance*, vol. 65, no. 3 (September): 401–426.

———. 2006. *The Calculus of Retirement Income*. Cambridge, UK: Cambridge University Press.

———. 2011. "What Does Retirement Really Cost?" *Research Magazine* (September): 1–5.

———. 2012. *The 7 Most Important Equations for Your Retirement*. Mississauga, ON, Canada: John Wiley & Sons.

———. 2013. *Life Annuities: An Optimal Product for Retirement Income*. Charlottesville, VA: CFA Institute Research Foundation.

Milevsky, Moshe A., Kwok Ho, and Chris Robinson. 1997. "Asset Allocation via the Conditional First Time Exit or How to Avoid Outliving Your Money." *Review of Quantitative Finance and Accounting*, vol. 9, no. 1 (July): 53–70.

Milevsky, Moshe A., and Huaxiong Huang. 2011. "Spending Retirement on Planet Vulcan: The Impact of Longevity Risk Aversion on Optimal Withdrawal Rates." *Financial Analysts Journal*, vol. 67, no. 2 (March/April): 45–58.

Milevsky, Moshe A., Kristen S. Moore, and Virginia R. Young. 2004. "Optimal Asset Allocation and Ruin-Minimization Annuitization Strategies: The Fixed Consumption Case." Working paper, University of Michigan (23 March): www.ifid.ca/Conference_Material/Moore_paper.pdf.

Milevsky, Moshe A., and Chris Robinson. 2005. "A Sustainable Spending Rate without Simulation." *Financial Analysts Journal*, vol. 61, no. 6 (November/December): 89–100.

Milevsky, Moshe A., and Virginia R. Young. 2002. "Optimal Asset Allocation and the Real Option to Delay Annuitization: It's Not Now-or-Never." Pensions Institute, Discussion Paper PI-0211 (1 September): www.pensions-institute.org/workingpapers/wp0211.pdf.

———. 2007. "Annuitization and Asset Allocation." *Journal of Economic Dynamics & Control*, vol. 31, no. 9 (September): 3138–3177.

Mitchell, John B. 2011. "Retirement Withdrawals: Preventive Reductions and Risk Management." *Financial Services Review*, vol. 20, no. 1 (Spring): 45–59.

Mitchell, Olivia S. 2001. "Developments in Decumulation: The Role of Annuity Products in Financing Retirement." NBER Working Paper 8567 (October).

Mitchell, Olivia S., James M. Poterba, Mark J. Warshawsky, and Jeffrey R. Brown. 1999. "New Evidence on the Money's Worth of Individual Annuities." *American Economic Review*, vol. 89, no. 5 (December): 1299–1318.

Munnell, Alicia H. 2008. "The Role of Government in Life-Cycle Saving and Investing." In *The Future of Life-Cycle Savings and Investing*, 2nd ed. Edited by Zvi Bodie, Dennis McLeavey, and Laurence B. Siegel. Charlottesville, VA: CFA Institute Research Foundation.

Nielson, Norma L. 2012. "Annuities and Your Nest Egg: Reforms to Promote Optimal Annuitization of Retirement Capital." C.D. Howe Institute, Commentary No. 358 (August).

Orszag, J. Michael. 2002a. "Discrete-Time Drawdown Analytics: Annuities and Drawdown in a Retirement Income Model." Watson Wyatt Technical Report 2002-RU04 (April).

———. 2002b. "Ruin in Retirement: Running Out of Money in Drawdown Programs." Watson Wyatt Technical Report 2002-TR-09 (December).

Pang, Gaobo. 2012. "Good Strategies for Wealth Management and Income Production in Retirement." In *Retirement Income: Risks and Strategies*. Edited by Mark J. Warshawsky. Cambridge, MA: MIT Press.

Pang, Gaobo, and Mark Warshawsky. 2010. "Optimizing the Equity-Bond-Annuity Portfolio in Retirement: The Impact of Uncertain Health Expenses." *Insurance, Mathematics & Economics*, vol. 46, no. 1 (February): 198–209.

Pharies, S. Andrew. 2010. "Primer on Commercial Annuities for Trusts and Estates Attorneys." *Estate Planning 2010.* Continuing Education of the Bar, California (http://www.ceb.com/info/es3160loutline.htm#chapter8).

Poterba, James M. 2001. "Annuity Markets and Retirement Security." Center for Retirement Research, Boston College (June).

Previtero, Alessandro. 2011. "Stock Market Returns and Annuitization: A Case of Myopic Extrapolation." Presented at the IFID Conference: Annuity Day 2011, Toronto (24 November).

Pye, Gordon B. 2012. *The Retirement Retrenchment Rule: When It's Too Late to Save More for Retirement.* New York: GBP Press.

Robinson, Chris, and Nabil Tahani. 2010. "Sustainable Retirement Income for the Socialite, the Gardener and the Uninsured." *Financial Services Review*, vol. 19, no. 3 (Fall): 187–202.

Scott, Jason S. 2008. "The Longevity Annuity: An Annuity for Everyone?" *Financial Analysts Journal*, vol. 64, no. 1 (January/February): 40–48.

Scott, Jason S., William F. Sharpe, and John G. Watson. 2009. "The 4% Rule—At What Price?" *Journal of Investment Management*, vol. 7, no. 3 (Third Quarter): 31–48.

Sell, Susan J., Steve P. Cooperstein, and Joel Jessen. 2004. "Retirement Income Solutions: Payout Annuities." Presented at Society of Actuaries, Spring Meeting, San Antonio, TX (14–15 June).

Sexauer, Stephen C., Michael W. Peskin, and Daniel Cassidy. 2012. "Making Retirement Income Last a Lifetime." *Financial Analysts Journal*, vol. 68, no. 1 (January/February): 74–84.

Sexauer, Stephen C., and Laurence B. Siegel. 2013. "A Pension Promise to Oneself." *Financial Analysts Journal*, vol. 69, no. 6 (November/December): 13–32.

Shankar, S. Gowri. 2009. "A New Strategy to Guarantee Retirement Income Using TIPS and Longevity Insurance." *Financial Services Review*, vol. 18, no. 1 (Spring): 53–68.

Shapiro, Arnold F. 2010. "Post-Retirement Financial Strategies from the Perspective of an Individual Who Is Approaching Retirement Age." Society of Actuaries, Pension Section (www.soa.org/files/research/projects/research-post-retire-fin-shapiro.pdf).

Sharpe, William F. 2007. *Investors and Markets: Portfolio Choices, Asset Prices, and Investment Advice.* Princeton, NJ: Princeton University Press.

Smith, Gary, and Donald P. Gould. 2007. "Measuring and Controlling Shortfall Risk in Retirement." *Journal of Investing*, vol. 16, no. 1 (Spring): 82–95.

Society of Actuaries. 2008. "Managing Post-Retirement Risks: A Guide to Retirement Planning." 2nd edition (October).

Spitzer, John J. 2008. "Retirement Withdrawals: An Analysis of the Benefits of Periodic 'Midcourse' Adjustments." *Financial Services Review*, vol. 17, no. 1 (Spring): 17–29.

Stabile, Gabriele. 2006. "Optimal Timing of the Annuity Purchase: Combined Stochastic Control and Optimal Stopping Problem." *International Journal of Theoretical and Applied Finance*, vol. 9, no. 2 (March): 151–170.

Stout, R. Gene. 2008. "Stochastic Optimization of Retirement Portfolio Asset Allocations and Withdrawals." *Financial Services Review*, vol. 17, no. 1 (Spring): 1–15.

Stout, R. Gene, and John B. Mitchell. 2006. "Dynamic Retirement Withdrawal Planning." *Financial Services Review*, vol. 15, no. 2 (Summer): 117–131.

Stutzer, Michael. 2003. "Asset Allocation Advice: Reconciling Expected Utility and Shortfall Risk." Working paper, Burridge Center for Securities Analysis and Valuation, University of Colorado, Boulder (December).

Tahani, Nabil, and Chris Robinson. 2010. "Freedom at 55 or Drudgery till 70?" *Financial Services Review*, vol. 19, no. 4 (Winter): 275–284.

Turner, John A., and Hazel A. Witte. 2009. "Retirement Planning Software and Post-Retirement Risks." Society of Actuaries and the Actuarial Foundation (December): www.soa.org/files/pdf/research-pen-retire-planning-soft.pdf.

Turra, Cassio M., and Olivia S. Mitchell. 2008. "The Impact of Health Status and Out-of-Pocket Medical Expenditures on Annuity Valuation." In *Recalibrating Retirement Spending and Saving*. Edited by John Ameriks and Olivia S. Mitchell. Oxford, UK: Oxford University Press.

Vanduffel, S., J. Dhaene, M. Goovaerts, and R. Kaas. 2003. "The Hurdle-Race Problem." *Insurance, Mathematics & Economics*, vol. 33, no. 2 (October): 405–413.

Venter, Gary G. 1983. "Utility with Decreasing Risk Aversion." *Proceedings & Casualty Actuarial Society*, vol. 70, no. 133/134: 144–155.

Waring, Barton M., and Laurence B. Siegel. 2015. "The Only Spending Rule Article You Will Ever Need." *Financial Analysts Journal*, vol. 71, no. 1 (January/February): 91–107.

Warshawsky, Mark J. 2012. "Recent Developments in Life Annuity Markets and Products." In *Retirement Income: Risks and Strategies*. Edited by Mark J. Warshawsky. Cambridge, MA: MIT Press.

Weinsier, David J. 2005. "Hot Topics in Fixed Annuities." *Society of Actuaries Record*, vol. 31, no. 1 (22–24 May): 1–26.

Williams, Duncan, and Michael Finke. 2011. "Determining Optimal Withdrawal Rates: An Economic Approach." *Retirement Management Journal*, vol. 1, no. 2 (Fall): 35–46.

Yaari, Menahem E. 1965. "Uncertain Lifetime, Life Insurance, and the Theory of the Consumer." *Review of Economic Studies*, vol. 32, no. 2 (April): 137–150.

Zahm, Nathan, and John Ameriks. 2012. "Estimating Internal Rates of Return on Income Annuities." Vanguard Center for Retirement Research (March).

Zwecher, Michael J. 2010. *Retirement Portfolios*. Hoboken, NJ: John Wiley & Sons, Inc.

RESEARCH FOUNDATION
CONTRIBUTION FORM

☑ **Yes**, I want the Research Foundation to continue to fund innovative research that advances the investment management profession. Please accept my tax-deductible contribution at the following level:

Thought Leadership Circle................ US$1,000,000 or more
Named Endowment....................... US$100,000 to US$999,999
Research Fellow .... US$10,000 to US$99,999
Contributing Donor........................ US$1,000 to US$9,999
Friend .... Up to US$999

I would like to donate $ _____ .

☐ My check is enclosed (payable to the CFA Institute Research Foundation).
☐ I would like to donate appreciated securities (send me information).
☐ Please charge my donation to my credit card.
　　　　　　■ VISA　■ MC　■ Amex　■ Diners

Card Number

___ / ___　　　　　　　_____
Expiration Date　　　　　Name on card　PLEASE PRINT

☐ Corporate Card
☐ Personal Card　　　　　_____
　　　　　　　　　　　　　Signature

☐ This is a pledge. Please bill me for my donation of $ _____
☐ I would like recognition of my donation to be:
　　■ Individual donation　■ Corporate donation　■ Different individual

_____
PLEASE PRINT NAME OR COMPANY NAME AS YOU WOULD LIKE IT TO APPEAR

PLEASE PRINT　☐ Mr.☐ Mrs.☐ Ms.　MEMBER NUMBER _____

_____
Last Name (Family Name)　　　　First　　　　Middle Initial

_____
Title

_____
Address

_____
City　　　　　State/Province　　Country ZIP/Postal Code

Please mail this completed form with your contribution to:
The CFA Institute Research Foundation • P.O. Box 2082
Charlottesville, VA 22902-2082 USA

For more on the CFA Institute Research Foundation, please visit www.cfainstitute.org/learning/foundation/Pages/index.aspx.

Made in the USA
Monee, IL
21 April 2021

66381415R00059